Praise for *"Just Fine, Thank You"*

I didn't grow up in poor, rural mid-America during the 1940s. I didn't grow up as a girl. I didn't grow up in a family marred by alcohol and dysfunction. Evelyn did. My emotions rode a roller coaster as I read about her childhood. Some of the stories are funny. Many of the stories are very sad. Some of the stories were painful. These are stories of perseverance—of despair leading to hope. They are stories that help put our own lives and future into perspective.

—Rev. Doug Diehl retired United Methodist Elder

A moving, poignant memoir about love, fear, guilt, and what's it's like for a child to love life and be in emotional pain at the same time. Leite shares what it's like to live in a closed family system with a 'no talk' rule and to struggle daily to make sense of craziness. She also shows how society works best when we share ourselves with other people, feel our real feelings and define ourselves as individuals.

—John C. Friel, Ph. D. Licensed Psychologist
in private practice in Minneapolis and Reno/Tahoe
New York Times bestselling author
of nine books including
Adult Children: The Secrets of Dysfunctional Families
and *The 7 Best Things (Happy) Couples Do*

In her powerful memoir, *"Just Fine Thank You,"* Evelyn Leite reveals the impact of adverse experiences on children occurring in the vacuum of denial. This vacuum is maintained thru silence, and because children, wanting to feel loved, learn to live in terror of revealing their forbidden feelings, worries, and fears, especially to their parents. Consequently, addictions may flourish behind the persona of a perfect family.

—Patricia Evans, Author of *The Verbally Abusive Relationship, Controlling People, and more*
www.verbalabuse.com

I have known Evelyn for ten years. I find her intriguing and amazing. Her early youth biography affirms my belief in the indomitability of the human spirit. I wait anxiously for the next books.

—Ronald Wick, Colorado Entrepreneur

This book gives great insight into the complexity of Leite's first thirteen years of life, a story of love, longings, humor and hope. The message to her: Give a perfect family face to the world always. The Farm and small town life without electricity and in-door plumbing are reminders of difficult, but often humorous challenges to daily chores and family entertainment.

—Sharon Whitney Retired Librarian

Evelyn Leite has captivated me with her personal story shared from her perspective for each age and year revealed. Beginning as a little girl, we enter into her world of processing to understand her family and life experiences—many of which specific to the era, while others, sadly, continue to this day for a great number of families. Highly relatable, entertaining, and poignant, *"Just Fine Thank You,"* is a book worthy of attaining a best seller's status.

—Rev. Pamela Christian, Author of award-winning *Faith to Live By* series, International Speaker, Radio/Television Host
https://PamelaChristianMinistries.com

"Just fine, thank you."

Growing up with family SECRETS

Evelyn M. Leite MHR, LPC

"Just Fine, Thank You"
Fourth book in the *Blood, Sex, and Tears* series.

Published by:
Living With Solutions
PO Box 9702
Rapid City, SD 57709
Copyright 2019 © by Evelyn M. Leite, MHR, LPC

ISBN: (sc) 978-1-733540964
        (eb) 978-1-733540971

Library of Congress: 9781733540964

Printed in the United States

Disclaimer

This is a personal document based on events which happen to people every day. They happened to me.

It is a story about alcoholism and pain, about faith and healing, and about joy and recovery. It is written that all people in the helping professions may gain insight into problems family members face when alcohol is destroying their lives. It is further written to bring love, hope, and inspiration to people trying to cope with a disease they do not understand. This book is published with permission of close family members. Some names and events are changed but the story is real and could be happening next door to you. Or in your house.

This book is designed to provide information about the subject matter covered. It is sold with the understanding that the publisher and authors are not engaged in rendering legal, accounting, or other professional services. If legal or other expert assistance is required, the services of a competent professional should be sought.

Every precaution has been taken in the development of this book to bring you accurate and up to date information. However, there may be mistakes both typographical and in content. Therefore, this text should be used only as a general guide and not as the ultimate source for improving family relations.

TABLE OF CONTENTS

Dedication   i
Introduction   iii
Preface   v

Chapter 1—Please Love Me   1
Chapter 2—Trying to Be Good   19
Chapter 3—You Stupid Girl   29
Chapter 4—Moving Again   35
Chapter 5—Life on the Farm   57
Chapter 6—What Farm Kids Do   67
Chapter 7—Summertime   77
Chapter 8—Ladies Aid   87
Chapter 9—The Apple   95
Chapter 10—Bad News   103
Chapter 11—A Dangerous Man   107
Chapter 12—Baby Jerry   129
Chapter 13—The Mystery Man   145
Chapter 14—Family   157
Chapter 15—Don't Tell   161
Chapter 16—In Love with Love   169
Chapter 17—The Big Freeze   173
Chapter 18—Visitors   185
Chapter 19—Watching My Back   189
Chapter 20—Moving On   195
Post Script   199
Author's Note   201

Dedication

This book is dedicated to my husband Allen J. Knapp and to my wonderful remaining brother, (who shall remain nameless to protect his identity). My brother and my husband are beautiful demonstrations of God's love and grace. They give me so much support.

And in loving memory of my father, Lon Jones, for whom understanding creates an indestructible bond; my mother Edith Jones, whom I love dearly and miss every day of my life; my deceased brothers whom I adore and miss terribly; and all my cherished aunts on both sides of the family who were such a great influence on my life. To my cousins, who also shall remain nameless to protect their identity, but who know who they are. They provided endless hours of fun and laughter and many of them still do.

Also to my amazing children Lonny, Robert, and Scott, God's greatest gift to me. They are wonderfully loving and successful people, not because of me, but in spite of my ignorance and as an apology to them for all the tears they shed because of my mental instability. And to my grandchildren who shall remain nameless, but who I hope know that I would give my life for them.

Introduction

This book is part of the *Blood, Sex, and Tears* series written to shed light on the myriad of complex issues facing families where addiction is present. Everyone suffers and they unwittingly pass the insanity on to future generations. I hope to give people insight into dysfunction and learn how to prevent it from continuing.

As a little girl growing up in the forties and fifties, I experienced life very differently from young people today. Outhouses, kerosene lamps, horse-drawn wagons, tube radios, and wood-burning stoves were the modern conveniences of the time.

The culture was very different with rules and secrets to uphold. Some rules I learned and was required to follow were:

- Children are to be seen and not heard.
- Children must earn their keep.
- All family business is extremely private.
- Parents or teachers are never wrong, even when they rage.
- Sex is never to be discussed.
- Pride in the family name must always be protected.
- God will punish all wrongdoers, including little children.
- No matter what is happening, or how you are feeling, if someone asks you how you are, the stock answer is, "Just fine, thank you."

Through my experiences and observations, I learned some men see little girls as sex toys, and alcohol makes people crazy. Since sex was never to be discussed, and parents or other adults are never wrong, I had to learn to process such things on my own.

As you read my story, I ask you to consider your own life and family to recognize any destructive dysfunction that has impaired you, and is likely adversely impacting your spouse and children, and potentially impacting generations to come. Family dysfunction always reveals itself in the children, progressing in greater degree from generation to generation. You can stop this destructive progression by the simple act of acknowledging truth. It's important to acknowledge that a family is only as healthy as its secrets and in our family there were many private things unsafe to discuss.

Preface

My mother met my father in 1929 when she and her family accompanied her sister, Eva, to the Tuberculosis Sanitarium south of Custer, South Dakota where my father was a cook. My father had brought his very sick young wife, Laura, to the sanitarium in 1927 where she died six months later. My mother, living in the east part of the state, and my father 300 miles away, built a long-distance relationship over a four-year period.

During these times, it was not easy to find steady work or money enough to bring his parents, sisters, and brothers from Missouri to South Dakota. But my father managed to do both. Some of the family left, after a time, longing for the more comfortable climate of Missouri. Two of Daddy's sisters found husbands and set up permanent residence in South Dakota.

My dad was a short, slim, dapper man with black hair, flashing blue-green eyes, a square-cut jaw, and a cleft chin. My mother fell for his southern charm, and his handsome, seductive bad-boy appeal. Dad thought himself indestructible, and would actually fight men twice his size. In his mind there was nothing he couldn't do. He handled women, model Ts, and horses with aplomb.

My mother was English aristocracy from a large family that saw its share of tragedy. Her ancestors came over on the Mayflower (or at least one of the first ships) and homesteaded their way across the country. My beautiful mother was blessed with blue, hooded eyes, and a china-doll face. Her brown, naturally-curly hair was magically always in place. She possessed a cool demeanor, and an elegant, refined sense of style, and spoke perfect English.

She was a 1920s flapper surrounded by adoring men. I still have pictures of some of those men, and I still own the peach silk dress she wore while doing the Charleston. She was eighteen when women fought for and won the right to vote, which she said meant everything to her.

Having money helped her go to college at a time when women were viewed as inferior and lacking in the brains department. In college she dated a highly popular American bandleader from North Dakota, but only a couple of times, because she said, "He was nice but boring."

In 1932 my mother and father had a grand formal wedding in my Granddaddy Jim's rose arbor beside his stately home in South Dakota. This was shortly after the stock market crash of 1929 which made my grandfather an even wealthier man. The dust bowl days of the 1930s along with the Great Depression gave my mother nightmares, while my banker grandfather was busy acquiring farms.

My dad said my grandfather made his first million by being an IRS informer, but no one really knew the truth of that. My older cousin, Bob, said our grandfather was a ruthless man who took what he wanted. To hear my mother talk, Granddaddy Jim was next to being a saint. To me he was pure love.

When my parents were young, they led very different lives. My dad, born in 1898, was working full time at the age of eleven in a sawmill to support his mother, two brothers, and three sisters. His dad was disabled at the same sawmill by an unfortunate run-in with a saw that made sure he'd never work again. Dad was never afraid of work. Despite his lack of education, he devoured newspapers, stayed up-to-date on politics, and fanatically stayed glued to war information broadcasts over the shortwave radio. He often lamented his regret for being "too old" to enlist after the Japanese struck Pearl Harbor in World War II.

Duty called my mother to drop out of college to take care of her younger brothers and sisters, and her mother who was dying. In her spare time, she helped run her dad's hardware store while he was busy at his bank. She also cooked and did laundry for her brothers.

Her small body contained a horrible secret. I didn't learn until after she died that she'd suffered with bulimia since she was fifteen. When I discovered this, a lot of things I'd never understood made sense. It was why she had no teeth, why *fat* was a dirty word, and why she had so much stomach trouble.

My mother was bedridden for months after my older brother was born, because of a doctor's carelessness. They said she might never walk again. Dad found a chiropractic manipulator who healed her—just in time to birth me. I think she must have been exhausted by the time I came along, even if I was only the second child in the family.

I was nicknamed Bubbles because I blew bubbles continuously for weeks after I was born. I also sucked my thumb until I was twelve years old—sometimes my only comfort. I am the only girl in a family that I thought only had six boys. Imagine my amazement at discovering there were two more boys older than me from prior relationships.

Dad always felt inferior to mother. He told us many times he could never figure out why she married him. Mom remained crazy about him long after he died. Dad killed his pain with alcohol. Mom killed hers with the Bible. I killed mine with a number of things—one of which was rage.

Because my father could be dazzling, generous, gentle, and unconquerable, I found good, honest men colorless and dull as I grew up. Dad and I increasingly had major rage contests—arguments and disagreements of grand proportion. He died feeling entirely blameless concerning his part of our relational dysfunction.

Growing up, the 1940s saw me struggling to survive. The fifties found me struggling to belong. The sixties found me seriously haunted.

Every member of a family has their own experiences and concepts of the family dynamics. This is mine and mine alone, and not necessarily those of my brothers. In the postscript I give you more details about the forces governing me and the teenage escapades awaiting me.

Chapter One

Please Love Me

I'm confused. *Why are we piling everything we own into Daddy's old truck? Where are we going?*

This log cabin is home. I like it up here on the mountain with all the birds and the deer peeking out from behind the trees.

Mama is rushing around, her light brown hair blowing in the breeze, her housedress flapping as she lugs a heavy box to the truck. She yells at me, "Get Mike and hold on to him; he's getting in the way."

Daddy is piling stuff in the back of the truck as I run over and grab my two-year old brother. He's almost as big as me and he doesn't want to be corralled. "Come on Mike, let's go see if there are any fish in the stream." Mike loves sitting at the edge of the stream that runs by our cabin and watching for fish to jump up out of the water. He usually scares them away because he likes to flap his hands in the cool blue stream.

Mike comes willingly and finds a place to sit and look for fish. Ted comes over to the log where I am sitting trying to keep Mike happy and says, "I know something you don't."

Before I can ask him what it is, Daddy yells at Ted, "Come help your mother carry those things out of the house." Ted runs to help. Ted probably knows where we are going. He's eighteen months older than my four years, and always knows things I don't. I'd be lost without Ted.

Are we leaving because of the mountain lion? It was screaming outside of our cabin window a couple nights ago. Mama's face turned white and she dropped the kettle of soup she was carrying to the supper table.

Ted said, "It's okay, Bubs, I'm not scared of any old mountain lion."

Mama was on her hands and knees mopping up the soup. She said, "He can't hurt us. He's outside and he can't get in here."

Then why is she so scared and where is my daddy?

When Daddy came in, she ran to him and said, "Oh thank God you are all right."

"Why?" he responded.

"Didn't you hear the mountain lions?"

"No, I just got home from hauling a load of logs down the mountain." Daddy looked tired. His thick black hair was full of wood chips.

Finally, the cabin is empty and the truck is loaded. Ted climbs up in the back with all the piled up stuff. Daddy checks to make sure he is sitting down in a small corner in front of the truck box and tells him, "You sit here and do not stand up. Pound on the back window if anything falls out. We don't have very far to go."

I crawl in the cab between Mama and Daddy and Mama gets in holding Mike. The truck sputters and spurts as Daddy grabs the gear shift. I have to move my

2

legs way over against Mama so he can pull down on the shift and get the truck in gear.

"Mama are we leaving because of the mountain lion?"

"No, we have to move to town so Ted can go to school. He starts in a few days."

"I want to go to school too."

"You will next year."

"Where are we going?"

"Custer."

I feel better. Custer, South Dakota is where Aunt Pearl lives. I've been there lots of times. I'm picturing my daddy's sister, Aunt Pearl, a round woman who moves around fast getting things done.

I really like her and her husband, Rob. He's a quiet man, thin like a string bean. Daddy says he "works for the WPA." I don't know what that means, but I've heard Daddy say, "No man worth his salt takes anything from the government." I can tell by Daddy's voice it is a bad thing.

Aunt Pearl and Uncle Rob live high on a hill and she has what Mama calls a brood of kids. The oldest, Roy, is blond and twenty-one and so handsome. Mama says he's a paratrooper and in the war. I'm not sure what that means. Glenn is next. He's eighteen, and clean and tidy, with a sweet smile. He's always good to me when he notices I'm around. Two girl cousins, Oleta and Ann, are next, and then Bobby, who is Ted's age. The youngest, Larry, is the same age as Mike.

3

I really like going to their loud and noisy house. The last time I was there Roy was home on something called "leave" from the army. My eyes got really big as Roy chased Oleta through the kitchen with an army boot in his hand. Aunt Pearl leaped up, her huge breasts heaving up and down, as she yelled, "Stop it!" at the top of her lungs. Aunt Pearl finally gave up when Roy had his sister on the kitchen floor making her tell him she was sorry for something.

Another time I saw Glenn and Ann wrestling on the grass, which proves to me "might makes right." I am crazy about Glenn. Maybe it's because he looks so much like Daddy, except one side of his handsome face has a big, purple mark in the shape of a hand. Daddy said it was because Aunt Pearl had seen something scary when she was pregnant and slapped her hand to her face, so Glenn was born with a handprint on his cheek.

Bobby teases me. "Why are you so quiet? Cat got your tongue?"

I shake my head.

"Are you bashful?"

My cheeks turn red, my eyes drop.

"Oh, look she's blushing."

I'm glad no one pays much attention to Bobby.

§

"Here we are," Daddy says. Our new home is a small, old-looking house that used to be white, with

a front porch that is sagging as if it's melting into
the ground.

I see three other dingy, droopy houses close by
with kids playing outside. I can tell Ted's excited.
"Look Bubs, there are other kids."

Daddy unlocks the door and we walk into cool empty
air that feels like it hasn't been breathed for a while. Our
footsteps and voices echo as Ted and I run from room to
room. The linoleum floor smells freshly waxed. It's bright
in here with no curtains at the windows. There is one
bedroom for Mama and Daddy off the kitchen, and a
dining room and a living room.

Ted and Mike's bed goes in the living room along
with a couch and dresser, my cot goes in the dining room
near the coal stove, the table and chairs go in the kitchen.

From the saggy back porch we can see a beautiful,
large white building that Mama says is a mortuary. It is
so close we can hear singing coming from it. "They must
be having a funeral today," Mama says.

Five or six kids from the other houses gather in our
front yard to watch Daddy and Glenn unload the truck.
They must be curious to see who their new neighbors
are.

Ann is in the house trying to help Mama organize
things and I'm trying to keep Mike under control. *Does
Mama see how good I'm being—how I'm trying to help her by
taking care of Mike?* I wonder if she sees me at all.

Ted's outside talking to the new kids. He is petting
their dog. I'm watching him through the dining room

window thinking, *Ted's been asking for a dog. I wonder if he will get one now.*

I stand on the edge of the group of kids outside and watch how easy it is for Ted to talk with the kids. David, a skinny little kid with freckles and big blue eyes, asks me, "Who are you?"

"That's my sister, Bubbles," Ted says.

"Going to school this week?" David asks.

"No, Mama says I have to wait 'til next year."

"Me too." David points to a kid in the middle of the group. "My big brother Doug is in second grade." David looks like he is wearing his brother's hand-me-down jeans. A big leather belt holds him together in the middle, but his jeans look about ready to fall off his skinny butt.

There is another kid there who has a big red wagon. His name is Jimmy. "Jump in," he tells me, "and I will give you a ride."

Jimmy's really nice, I think as he pulls me around the yard.

All the houses are clumped together close. The people who live here share an outhouse, a small wooden building covered with tar paper. I check it out and inside I see a bench with three huge holes sawed in it, and a little wooden stool for climbing up to the bench. The floppy wooden door is hard to pull shut, so it hangs open a little as I use the outhouse.

Some of my cousins say *pee,* but Mama would never let me use that word. *Boy, it really stinks in here. I got to get out of here as fast as I can. What if somebody comes? I could fall in this hole and down into the stinky slop. No one would know where I am.*

It's hard doing my business while I hang on tight to a board that runs along the side of the wall. My short legs dangle down the front of the high bench. I can hear voices out there, and I feel scared. *Please, nobody come in here.*

A couple days after we move in, I slide off the seat of the outhouse. *Oh, no, my bottom hurts!* I can barely pull up my underpants because there's a big sliver sticking out down there. I wobble to the house as fast as I can. "Mama, I have a big sliver down there."

"Where?"

"Down there!"

Mama sends everybody out of the house, pulls all the shades, puts the kitchen chair right under the bright lightbulb in the middle of the kitchen ceiling, turns me over on her lap, and digs out the sliver with a needle.

Why, does everybody have to leave? Why did Mama pull the shades? Is this a secret? Did I do something wrong? Is this something bad? All these thoughts fly through my head, as I try my best to keep from screaming bloody murder while Mama digs out the sliver with a needle. Finally, I give in and a ragged cry comes out of my throat.

"All done now," Mama says, "Stop crying, you're just fine."

§

I feel lost. Ted's in the first grade and I don't have him to play with, or to explain things to me. On his way home the first day of school, he brings home a stray dog with sad eyes. He's so excited. "Can I keep him? Please Mama, can I keep him?" He runs around the kitchen looking for food he can feed the dog.

The next day Ted brings home another one. "Alley Oop," (that's what Daddy calls Ted, after the funny book character) "you have to stop bringing home all these dogs. We can't feed them."

One afternoon Ted brings home a dog that looks just like Lassie. When I see him I just love him. I bury my face in the collie's hair and secretly claim him for my own.

"Let's name him Prince," Ted says.

Daddy makes Ted take all of the other dogs back where he found them, but at least we get to keep Prince. "I cried when I had to leave them. They looked so sad," Ted said.

Prince is our constant companion. He stands patiently while Mike and I roll around on him, tie ribbons to his tail, and put make-believe saddles on his back. We use him as a horse to pull the wagon with my dolls in it.

Daddy brings home bones from the downtown grocery store where he works cutting meat. First Mama makes soup out of them, then Prince gets them.

The squeaky side door off the kitchen of our house opens to our saggy back porch, and an ugly, dirt yard without trees. This is where Mike and I make mud pies.

From here we can see the thick green grass at the mortuary. There are shrubs over there with pinkish-purply flowers, and some tired yellow rose bushes by the concrete steps.

I think the front door of the funeral home is the most beautiful thing I've ever seen. *Why can't we have a door like that?* The door is made of greenish metal with golden angels perched on each side of the gold door handles that shine when the sun hits them.

Daddy says it's now Indian summer. "They call it that when it turns cold around Labor Day and then turns warm again."

I heard a lady ask my mother, "Aren't you afraid to live by a mortuary?"

Mama seemed so sure when she answered, "Ghosts won't hurt you. It's real people you have to watch out for." I guess ghosts are nothing to be afraid of.

Harvey is the man who works at the mortuary. Daddy says he is the groundskeeper. "Stay out of his way and don't make him mad," he says. Harvey's ears stick out under his worn-out felt hat. He wears a faded plaid shirt and green pants that look like they've been washed a lot.

Harvey yells, "Stay off the grass," at us kids when we try to roll in the thick green front yard. But he lets us play on the back lawn and run up and down the stairs that go down to the place where the bodies and coffins are kept. A concrete wall is above the back steps that go down to the cellar. Ted says from the grass it is only two feet high, but from the bottom of the steps it might be six feet. It is perfect for jumping off on the grass and wide enough to balance on.

Old Harvey, putters around the mortuary all day long, slowly pushing his wheelbarrow full of weeds or dirt, or doing something with the flowers down on his knees. He grumbles about us kids "messing up his grass." He says, "You kids better watch out. If you fall backward off them steps you could break your head open and leave blood all over that I'd have to clean up." He speaks in a funny way and Daddy says he is Norwegian or something. But Harvey gives us suckers. David and I go over there every day.

§

Something is wrong with Mama. She lies down a lot. "Play with Mike a while," she tells me, "I have a bad headache."

I try to wait on her. Sometimes she'll let me bring her a glass of water, but mostly she says, "Just leave me alone." Mike and I tiptoe around in her dark room where she is lying on a bed with a cloth on her head.

Is she going to die? I don't dare ask her. I remember when Mama's brother died. He looked so strange lying in that rose-colored box.

"Just go play quietly with Mike. And don't go over to the mortuary. Stay in the house."

We play in the half-dark at the foot of her bed doing our best to wait quietly for Ted and Daddy to come

10

home. I shush Mike when he gets too excited playing with his cars.

Ted comes home from school and we sit in the kitchen looking at his schoolwork. He likes to show me what he's doing. "I will teach you what I know," he says. "But you probably won't get it."

Am I dumb like Ted says I am?

When Daddy walks in from work at night, I always race to meet him at the door. So does Mike, and both of us wrap our arms around his legs and yell, "Daddy, Daddy." He peels us off his legs and goes to check on Mama.

"You gotta take good care of Mama," he says to me. "She needs our help." Lots of times when Mama is sick, we can't go outside, because it's cold and snowing. Daddy comes home at lunchtime and puts more coal in the stove to keep us warm.

I am learning to make lunch. "You are such a big girl and you are doing such a good job," Daddy says.

"Does Mama have another headache?" I ask one morning as I wander sleepily to the kitchen. Daddy, with his hat on his head, and a dish towel slung over his shoulder, is fixing our breakfast. As he pours milk on my cereal he says, "No, she's over at old Alma's. You have a brother. Cousin Ann is coming to stay with you. I have to go to work."

A new baby brother? Where did he come from? What's he look like? What's his name?

Ann walks in as Daddy is leaving. I want to talk but she says, "Just eat your cereal. I have to help Mike get

11

dressed." Pretty, cheerful Ann never says anything mean to me. I'm kind of afraid and really excited as I ask her, "Why do we have a new baby brother? Where did he come from? Why is Mama gone? When will Mama be home?"

"You'll have to ask your Mama," is all Ann says to me.

§

"Come on kids, we are going to see your mother," Daddy says. At old Alma's house we visit Mama and see our tiny, new baby brother.

"His name is William, but we're going to call him Bill," Mama says. She is smiling and pointing to her cheek to be kissed. With tears in her eyes, Mama looks at Daddy and says, "Bill has a clubfoot."

I don't know what that means. He looks perfect to me all snuggly in a little white blanket.

When the doctor comes in Daddy says, "You kids go wait in the hall."

When we come back in, Mama says, "Bill has to go to the hospital to get his foot fixed, so I won't be home for a few more days. Be good for Daddy and Ann."

Nooo! I want my Mama.

§

I'm covered with snow from trying to make a snowman and so is Mike. The sun is shining for the first time in a week. Daddy drives up, dashes around, and opens the door of the car for Mama. She hands him a bundle of baby blankets and climbs out of the car in her brown fur coat. Mama always looks like a queen. Daddy is carrying Bill in the house.

Bill is perfect and sweet smelling with lots of blonde fluff on his little head. I get to hold him until he cries and then Mama puts him in the baby basket set up near my cot in the dining room.

I love Bill, but I miss Mama. "Daddy, when is Mama gonna have time for me?"

"Don't be so selfish," Daddy says, "your mama has had a hard time and has been very sick."

"Yeah, Bubs" Ted says, "Don't be so selfish."

I'm a terrible person. I feel sick. My stomach hurts.

Daddy makes supper and I am proud to carry a tray to Mama. He's right behind me with the coffee and water. She smiles weakly and says, "Thank you, Bubbles. Be sure to help Daddy, he needs you."

Can't Mama see I am helping Daddy?

Sometimes Ann comes and stays with us for a few hours or takes us to the movies on Saturday afternoons. "Mama don't make me go to the movies with Ann," I beg one Saturday. "I want to stay home with you."

Why can't I be with Mama all by myself? Bill gets to be home with Mama.

But she puts my jacket over my shoulders and gives me a gentle nudge out the door. It is some black-and-white movie with cowboys and Indians, and I hate it. I curl up in my seat and go to sleep sucking my thumb.

Ann wakes me up when the movie is over and we walk the few blocks home in the almost dark.

Mama is so close but she has no time for me and I get even more lonely for her. If she isn't washing diapers on a scrub board in a tin bathtub on the porch, she is boiling bottles and nipples in an old pan on top of the stove to sterilize them, or she's washing floors on her hands and knees, or ironing Daddy's shirts, or cooking. I help her hang diapers on the clothesline every day, climbing up on a little stool to reach the wire, putting the clothespins in my mouth the way Mama does, flipping a diaper over the wire, and fastening it neatly with two of the pins. Then I move the stool and do it again until I get to the end of the line. It feels good to help Mama. *Does she notice what a good girl I am being?* I'm trying hard not to be selfish.

At least it's spring and the diapers aren't freezing on the clothesline any more.

Ted is just home from school and we are wrestling in the living room when Mama says, "It's raining" and runs out the door to get the clothes off the line. I jump up and holler, "Come on Ted we have to help Mama."

"Nah," he says, "boys don't do girl's work." On the way out to the clothesline I tell Mama, "Ted's such a snot."

The crack of her hand comes across my face fast. "Don't say that word."

Holding my hand to my cheek I reel down the path heading toward the outhouse. *What's wrong with snot?*

Daddy says it all the time. I have to get away from her. I have to be alone.

Daddy is just getting home and sees me. "What's the matter, sweetheart?"

"Mama slapped me."

Pulling my hand away from my face he kisses my tears away and asks, "What did you do?"

"I said the word snot."

"She didn't mean it. She's just tired. You go back and tell her you're sorry."

Dutifully trudging to the kitchen with my head down, I whimper, "I'm sorry, Mama." I don't know if she hears me. She's folding diapers and hanging the damp ones over the back of chairs near the stove.

§

One cloudy, drizzly afternoon Mama has a headache and she's taking a nap with Bill and Mike. I wander outside and find David kicking a can around in his yard. "What ya doin?" I ask.

"Nothin'."

"Do you want to go over to the morgue and play?" I say.

Breaking into a run, he tosses back a "Beat ya!" and he's jumping off the wall by the time I get there. My little pink jacket isn't keeping me very warm and I'm shivery cold.

Harvey parks his wheelbarrow, and walks over. "You guys want ta see the caskets?"

"Yes!" David says, all excited and jumping up and down. "We want to see the caskets." David dances around with a big grin on his face. Just as I always do what Ted wants, I go along with David. "Come on then," Harvey says as he picks me up to carry me to the basement. At first, it feels good to be next to a warm body even though Harvey has a sour smell of dirt, tobacco spit, and old sweat that makes my nose sting.

David follows close behind us. "Are there dead people down here?" he asks.

"Yep," Harvey says, "but they won't hurt you."

Harvey pulls out a key and pushes the big double doors open to a cold, black concrete room with rows and rows of beautifully carved caskets, some closed, some open wide with white satin linings. It smells funny and awful.

It feels icky being held by Harvey. "I want down." I wiggle to get free so I can chase David who is running from one casket to another.

"There's a body in that one." David's eyes are wide as he points to the back of the room.

But Harvey doesn't put me down. He holds me tightly in his arms, and his dirty gray hands with mud under his fingernails creeps inside my jacket, and down inside my underpants into the place between my legs.

I'm afraid. It feels dirty and wrong and I try to get away from Harvey. *Why is he doing this? It feels awful. Let me down you—you snot.* Embarrassed and troubled I yell, "David, I have to go home."

16

"Okay, okay," David yells back. Then he looks at Harvey and asks, "Can we come back down here again? This is swell."

"Sure can. "Harvey says, boosting me up on his shoulders with my legs around his neck.

He stoops to walk through the door into the open and sets me down while he pulls the big double doors shut. I scamper up the steps and run as fast as I can to my house while David yells, "Wait, wait!" My nose is filled with the stink of Harvey as I crash into the kitchen through the side door.

"Quiet, Bill's still asleep."

Should I tell Mama what just happened? What happened anyway? Was it wrong? Why do I feel so bad? Am I a bad girl?

Mama is washing dishes and I'm doing my best to dry them when I say, "Harvey showed us the caskets in the cellar today. He said there were dead people in the basement. And he picked me up and rubbed his dirty hands between my legs . . . under my underpants."

She is busy but stops and looks at me. "You stay away from him. You don't need to go over there anyway." She walks away and leaves me in the kitchen alone.

An uneasy feeling churns in my stomach. I hit myself in the head and tell myself, *You are making something out of nothing again. Mama is right.* Whenever I complain or whine, I am told, "Stop making something out of nothing."

17

I find Prince and bury my face in his soft fur. His strong, warm body next to me makes me feel safe and cozy.

Chapter Two

Trying to Be Good

That night at supper, Daddy is excited. "Grandma, is coming to visit." I'd seen my daddy's mama once before and she was nice to me. *I hope she will hold me when she comes.* I ache to be loved. *I feel so strange, what is wrong with me?*

The next morning the air in our kitchen still smells like pancakes when I press my nose against the frosty kitchen window. I look toward town as far as I can see, watching the sidewalk for my grandma. I see my daddy walking toward work in the snow, then I can't see him anymore.

"What are you doing by the window?" Mama asks.

"Watching for Grandma." I want to be held. It feels like a hungry monster inside every part of me. *Grandma will rock me. She will love me, I just know it.*

"She's not going to be here for another week. Here, hold the baby while I fix his bottle." When I hold Bill it helps me feel better. Still, I need somebody to hold me. Grandma is my only hope, and I watch for her every day.

At last I see a stooped over little woman who looks like a bird in a black dress walk up the sidewalk on Daddy's arm. My heart is so happy as I run to her and hold her hand as we go into the house.

19

Almost as soon as Grandma gets in the house, Mama hands her three-year-old Mike who is sick, moaning, white-faced, and fussy. Grandma sits in the rocking chair and holds him all evening and then all the next day and every day she's here. Daddy says Mike has pneumonia and he rushes home at night to help Mama hold him under a sheet with a steaming pan of water with some awful smelling stuff floating in it.

I hang back and watch, my skinny bones aching to be next to a warm body with arms and a lap. Grandma does pay me attention, but it's just to give me things to do. "Go get me a blanket." "Go get me a washcloth." "Go tell your mother I need her." "Go get me a drink of water." "Be a good girl and keep Bill quiet. I finally got Mike to sleep."

"Is Mike going to die?" I asked my mama.

"Don't say that. What's the matter with you?"

I must just be bad.

Grandma leaves and so does my hope to be close to her and held by her.

It seems like it takes forever for Mike to get well. Daddy says, "He's not out of the woods yet," whatever that means.

I'm trying really hard to be good and not selfish.

§

Across the street from our house is a church we go to sometimes. I like dressing up in my pretty flowered dress with clean white tights, black patent-leather shoes and a hat with ribbons hanging down the back. Daddy always says, "There's my beautiful girl." That makes me feel proud of the way I look.

Ted wears a white shirt and a snazzy bow tie and his best black pants, and Mike wears short pants and knee socks. Mike hates those short pants. He complains every Sunday. "I want to wear man pants," but nobody listens.

Mama always wears her pink lace dress with ruffles on the collar, and a wide-brimmed hat with a veil. Wherever she goes the sweet smell of flowers goes with her. Daddy says Mama is the most beautiful woman in the world.

She is so pretty. Will I ever look like her?

Mama carries the baby in her arms and has a diaper thrown over her shoulder that sort of crumples the ruffles. Mama says Daddy is "dapper" as she fixes his tie and kisses him on the lips. He wears his hat tilted to one side, and has a sideways grin on his handsome face.

I'm so proud that you are my daddy. I love you so much. I want to tell him this but instead I hang on to his hand for dear life.

Church is boring. It's hard for me to sit still. *I'm hungry.* I wonder what we are going to have for dinner. I wonder what we will do this afternoon. Will we go for a ride in the hills or go up to Aunt Pearl's house? I wish the minister would hurry up.

§

"Who is God?" I ask Mama one day.

"He's who we pray to before going to sleep and at the table before eating our food."

"Is He nice?" I ask.

"He's nice to good kids."

He probably doesn't like me very much because I'm always in trouble.

One evening, I wake up to a strange man bending over me. I hear Mama's voice talking to him. "I don't know what's wrong Doctor," she says. "She's just been so listless, and sleepy all day." I feel the doctor place the thing he carries around his neck on my chest. He checks to see if I have a fever. "I can't find anything wrong with her. As he puts his stuff away in a black bag, he tells her, "Just give her a tablespoon of sugar with a few drops of kerosene on it and that'll fix her right up." I gag on the sugar with kerosene, but I make sure to get up and move around.

§

In the early summer we celebrate my sixth birthday with a picnic on a grassy hill beside a cold mountain stream. Aunt Pearl and some of her kids are here. Mama brings fried chicken and potato salad and a really pretty cake with candles. I see presents too. *I am so excited.* Aunt Pearl opens up covered dishes of beans and coleslaw, Jell-O and jars of pickles.

After we eat, everybody is full and groaning. It's almost time to cut the cake and open my presents.

Nobody is watching Mike. He wanders over to the stream and falls in the rushing water and is washed down almost through a culvert, where Daddy says he could get caught and drown.

Daddy jumps in with his shoes on and pulls him coughing and sputtering out of the water and onto the grassy bank. Mama rushes to wrap him in a towel and someone gives him water to drink

"We have to go home," Daddy says, "Mike will catch pneumonia."

"You can open your presents at home," Mama says as she and Aunt Pearl hurriedly pack up.

But it's my birthday. Well okay, Mike wins again.

§

Out of the blue, right in the middle of supper one night, a loud wailing siren goes off, blasting, whining, and shrieking on and on and on. Something clutches my chest and I feel like I can't breathe. *What is it?* Mama jumps up and herds us all into the living room and Daddy shuts off all the lights. We huddle together on the couch in the dark while our supper sits half-eaten on the table. Fear hangs like a cloud in the air.

"Mama, I'm scared," somebody says. *Is it me?*

Mama, holding Bill, whispers, "Shush everybody. Be quiet as a mouse. Don't talk." I can hear the sounds of our breathing, smell my daddy's Aqua Velva shaving lotion and feel Ted sitting next to me. We wait and wait and wait, fidgeting in the dark.

"Don't be afraid," Daddy whispers.

"I ain't afraid," Ted whispers back.

"We don't use the word ain't," Mama says in a quiet voice.

Finally, we hear another siren. "All clear," Daddy says as he jumps up to turn on the lights.

"What *was* that?" Ted asked when we get back to the table. Mama is warming up the cold food on the woodstove.

"It was a blackout," Daddy says. "We have to practice so if the enemy flies over they won't be able to see that there is a town below them. Blackouts will happen a lot now."

"Why?" I ask.

Ted answers, "Because we are in a war, stupid."

I don't dare ask, "What's a war?"

§

I can hear Mama and Daddy talking about the war at the kitchen table. Daddy is swearing. *It must be something really bad.*

I don't have much time to think about it. My first day of school is tomorrow. I need to pick out what I am going to wear and get my pencil and my Big Chief tablet ready to go. When I go to bed I can't sleep because I'm so excited about going to school.

On my very first day of school I skip along beside Ted, full of excitement. At last I am going to see what he does all day. Both of us are scrubbed and brushed sparkly clean. Mama has braided my hair so tight it pulls the skin on my face. At the end of the braids are bright new ribbons matching the colored figures in my new cotton pinafore. I stomp happily out the door in my new black shoes and white tights, proudly carrying a bag Mama made for me.

In the bag is a new box of crayons that are all my own. I don't have to share them with anybody.

At my classroom, my stomach is in knots and I want to go home. I wheel around to run but I see Ted disappear down the hall. I am trapped. Tears threaten to drip from my eyes.

A big, jolly woman with fat rolls up and down both sides of her body takes me by the shoulders. "I am Miss Goody, your teacher. What's your name?"

"Evelyn, but everybody calls me Bubbles."

"Well, I am going to call you Evelyn."

I like Miss Goody right off. I'm not afraid anymore when I see David walk in the door. We walk home from school together every day. We laugh and play, sometimes stopping to climb up and walk on a brick wall that goes around a building we pass on our way home.

All is well until the first snow, when David grabs a handful of the wet freezing stuff and washes my face with it. "Stop! Stop, you stupid snot," I yell.

"Stupid am I?" He grabs another handful of snow and rubs it in my eyes so icy water drips from my chin.

Why is he doing this? My heart twists with jagged hurt as he runs away laughing. "Come and get me," he yells as he runs home.

Now I am alone and confused. *I will get even with you. You better watch out.* "I don't like you anymore," I yell.

When I tell Mama what David did, she says, "Boys will be boys." She says that when I complain about Ted too.

§

School is a happy place, even with so much to do. I try so hard to please Miss Goody in art, reading, and arithmetic. Every gold star, every A, every pat on the back makes me proud, and I try even harder. One day during recess when most everyone, including Miss Goody is out of the room, Sally says, "Hey, she's gone. Let's look at our report cards."

Miss Goody walks in and catches us with our hands in her desk drawer. "What are you girls doing?" Her angry look makes a deep twinge in my chest.

"How could you do that?" she yells. "You're going to get an F from me now."

Ted is right. I am dumb as a post because I didn't even know we were doing anything wrong. When recess is over all the other kids laugh at us when we have to stand in the front of the room as school goes on as usual.

§

"Are you going to the rally tonight?" David asks me a few days later on our way home from school.

"What is a rally?"

"It's a place where everybody in town goes, and there is a big bonfire with lots of music and food, and somebody there sells war bonds. We always go."

"Never heard of it,"

"You must live under a rock."

Why does David know what a rally is and I don't?

When I get home I find Mama and ask, "Mama, do we have war bonds?"

She looks at me and says, "Why do you ask?"

"Because David's family has war bonds and they go to a rally."

"Not everybody can afford war bonds," she says. "We have all we can do to buy the rations we need to feed us."

"Rations? What are rations?"

"We have to use stamps to buy gas and sugar and shoes and other things because of the war."

I'm still not sure what a war is.

Chapter Three

You Stupid Girl

Daddy stands by the door with his hat on, waiting for Mama. I wrap my arms around his legs. "Where are you going?"

"We have to go to a funeral, sweetheart. Don't worry, Mrs. Brown is coming to stay with you. I'm depending on you to help her take care of the boys. You make sure Ted doesn't do anything stupid or bring home anymore dogs."

"When are you coming back?" I'm afraid. I want Daddy here in case something bad happens. *What if we have another blackout?* We've had about three now and my heart sits in my throat every time.

Fat old Mrs. Brown comes with her stinky armpits and plops in a chair as soon as Mama and Daddy leave. She reads stories to Mike and Bill.

Every time she tells Ted to do something, he looks at me, and asks, "Do I have to?" It makes me feel like I'm in charge.

I take Mama's pillow to bed with me and curl up with the sweet, perfumey smell of her. My arms and legs have itchy bumps all over them. *Should I tell Mrs. Brown about them? No, I'll just ignore them and maybe they will go away.*

Mama and Daddy get back late on Sunday afternoon. I am so happy to see them. Everybody rushes for Mama while Daddy pays Mrs. Brown.

"Were the kids good?" Daddy asks.

"Yes," Mrs. Brown says, "but Bubbles is a pill and she and Ted are quite a pair."

I look toward Mama but there is no chance of getting close to her with Mike on one side and Bill on the other. I throw my arms around Daddy's legs. He gives me a short hug and untangles. "I gotta go unload the car. Want to help me, Ted?"

§

It's a warmish, boring afternoon and I sit alone on our sagging back porch in the sun. The itchy bumps on my legs are driving me crazy. I slowly scrape the bumps off my legs with a butcher knife I'd found on the counter in the kitchen. It hurts, but the hurt kind of makes my stomach feel good. When my legs start to bleed I go in the house and show them to Mama.

She shrieks, "You stupid, stupid girl. What are you thinking? Go sit in that chair and don't get up until your dad gets home."

She hands me a bottle of yellow Chamberlain lotion and says, "Here. Rub this lotion on your legs." The lotion stings my legs and brings tears to my eyes. Ashamed and feeling like a pile of poop, I sit in the hard kitchen chair with its paint peeling off, pull off more paint with my stubby fingernails while I watch Mama fix supper.

"Go see what your little brother needs."

I can hear Mike yelling for her from the other room. Ted probably has Mike in a headlock again. He wrestles with the boys at school and practices on us. I leap in to rescue Mike and get punched for my effort. The blood from my legs is on the linoleum. Ted stops and asks, "What happened to you?"

"Nuthin'." *You wouldn't understand. You would just tell me how stupid I am again.*

§

It's winter and we are eating supper. Daddy isn't home yet. When sounds of screaming come from outside, we jump up from the table and run out in the chilly almost dark to see where the noise is coming from.

Two women are standing at the side of Jimmy's house looking at a cellar door.

When we walk over, we see Jimmy's head is sticking out through a hole in the cellar door, his eyes are bugged out, and his face is a sick purple-green in the glow of his mother's flashlight.

"What happened to him?" Mama asked.

"He was sent to the cellar for being bad," one of the women replied.

"How long has he been down there?" Mama asked.

"Most all day. He kept screaming to come up and finally he just tried to get out by himself. At this she started shrieking again. "I think he's dead."

31

I hear the scream of the ambulance siren as mama turns and marches us back into our own house. I never see Jimmy again. I dream about him though—that tough boy we played with, the one who pulled us in his wagon. Sometimes in my mind I see a picture of him; his buggy eyes and purple face haunt me. I don't think that either my Mama or my Daddy would never lock me in a cellar. *What did Jimmy do that was so bad?* The question torments me. When I ask Mama about it, she says, "Just don't think about it."

§

Just after supper, a few days before Christmas, we are playing cowboy in the living room. Ted and I, down on all fours, are the horses. We whinny and toss our heads and buck as hard as we can while Mike and Bill try to ride on our backs. We hear Mama yelling from the kitchen. She sounds excited. "Kids, come here. Look! Look! Look out the window."

My heart leaps and my eyes glaze over at the sight of Santa Claus peeking in the kitchen window at us. I don't know what to do. My stomach feels like its full of butterflies and I try to catch my breath.

Mama grabs Bill and brings him closer to the window. Mike is already banging on it hard. But Ted backs clear across the room because he isn't thrilled to see Santa. "Do you think he knows about the window I broke?" he asks me later, his blue eyes afraid. We all know if we are bad, Santa will put coal in our stockings. Mama has said that a million times.

When Daddy comes home a few minutes later I can't wait to tell him all about Santa. I climb on his lap, ruffle his thick black hair, and run my hands over the whiskers on his chin. Mama turns from doing something at the cupboard and jerks me off his lap, sending me sprawling across the floor.

"Ladies don't go barefoot. Go get your slippers on," she says.

My heart feels like it splits and I'm ashamed as I go to find my slippers. *Where did I leave them? My feet are really ugly. I should of had my slippers on.* Part of me is peeking around the door at Daddy and part of me is looking for my slippers.

Chapter Four

Moving Again

The snow this spring afternoon is just right for us to build the perfect snowman. As soon as I get home from school, Mama bundles both Mike and Bill up in wool plaid jackets, puffy snow-pants, and rubber overshoes. Their little eyes are shining out over Mama's scarves tied around their mouths and noses.

We roll, push, and tap the snow until we have a cold white ball of a body bigger than all three of us. Then we make a round stomach and we struggle to lift the frozen blob. It is hard and we almost lose it but finally we get it plopped on top of the body. The head that sort of looks like a ball of dirty dough comes easier.

"Go search for sticks to make arms and legs," I tell the boys. Bill waddles in his bulky clothes to the woodpile and shouts, "I got the arms." The sticks are almost longer than his two-year old self as he drags them along behind him.

Mike is waving a handful of coal that he got from beside the house. "I got the eyes and mouth," he shouts to Bill. His scarf is falling down around his neck, the snow is soaking through his snowsuit but he doesn't seem to notice.

I grab a corncob out of the woodbin for the nose. "Now we just need a pipe and maybe one of Daddy's old hats," I say.

Just then I look up and see Mama's daddy, Granddaddy Jim, and Mama's younger sister, Helen, walking down the street toward our house. I know who they are, they've been here before. Aunt Helen is beautiful in a fur coat that almost sweeps the sidewalk, her long reddish hair blowing in the wind. She holds a brown leather purse at her side with her tan gloved hands. *Where are her kids?* Granddaddy Jim puts his finger to his lips to shush me and I watch as they walk into the house. I hear my mama scream in delight.

From my little cot that night I listen hard to hear what Mama and Daddy are talking about with Granddaddy Jim, but I can't tell what they're saying. The next morning while I'm in school, Granddaddy Jim and Aunt Helen leave.

A couple of days later, I race in the house after school looking for Prince, who is usually waiting for us by the door. I call, "Prince, Prince," over and over, but no Prince. *When Ted gets home, he will find him.*

Ted whistles and calls for our dog Prince but he doesn't come.

"We can't find Prince anywhere," I say to Mama.

"You'll have to ask your Dad about him," she says.

Oh, oh. My stomach dips to my shoes. *This isn't good.*

"Gave him away," Daddy says at supper. "Can't take him with us." When Ted starts to cry, Daddy says, "Be a man."

36

I swallow my tears. *Not Prince!*

Ted squeaks out, "Why? What're we doin'?"

"We're moving to Seneca. Granddaddy Jim needs us," Mama says.

Why are we moving to where Granddaddy Jim lives? What does he need us for? I choke down my food the best I can and tell myself I will never love another dog.

At school a few days later, I don't say good-bye to Miss Goody. "See you tomorrow," I say brightly with a fake smile.

The next morning in the dark, cold dawn, Mama rolls us out of bed. "Here, put these on," she says, handing us our clothes. Groggy, I drag on the dress and sweater and pull on a pair of Ted's outgrown long pants under my dress to keep my legs warm.

"Now go help Mike," she tells me.

When we are dressed, Daddy herds his sleepy brood to the truck in the dark, sticking us in the cab on top of each other, and throwing our old black suitcases and some boxes in the back.

The depot at the train station is full of light and people are bustling around the ticket counter or waiting on wooden benches. Mama has on her best housedress and her glossy-brown fur coat. On her feet she wears the snakeskin leather high heels that she usually only wears to church. "I wore these shoes when we got married," she tells me proudly every time she puts them on. Every one of her brown hairs is in place, held there by a fur pill-box hat.

"I'll see you in a couple of days," Daddy says when we get to our seats on the train. When he kisses me good-bye I smell his special, wonderful smell. "Help your mama," he says. I want to hang on to him and never let go.

Chug-alacka, chug-alacka, chug-alacka. The endless noise of the train on the tracks changes to a high-pitched piercing squeal of metal on metal. Every time we slow to a crawl going through a town the loud train whistle hurts my ears. Finally with a big screech we stop in front of a small gray, weathered building with a weathered board porch. There are people sitting on a single narrow bench in front of the wood door with its peeling red paint. My neck hurts and my head is throbbing from bumping against the arm of the seat.

"I'm so hungry my stomach thinks my throat's been cut," Ted says, rubbing his stomach.

"Ted, that's crude!" Mama says, trying to look shocked but I see the little smile on her face. Ted never really does anything wrong in Mama's eyes.

Aunt Helen is waiting for us at the train station, with Granddaddy Jim's big brown Buick. Mama hands me Bill as I crawl in the back seat between Ted and Mike. Mama's rubbing her neck and forehead. *Is she having another bad headache? Daddy says I have to take care of her. What can I do?*

We drive along bumpy gravel streets covered with sooty, melting snow, past shabby gray buildings and small brick stores, and yards with no trees, and old cars. As we drive through town, Aunt Helen points out things to Mama. "See there's Jack Bruce's new store. He must be making lots of money, he just built an apartment on the back of his store and a new room for produce. You should have married him Edith."

I look sharply at Aunt Helen and think, *What do you mean, you witch? There's nobody better than my daddy.*

"Look there's Rosland's Cafe. Old Roy just built this for Ellen and her new husband. She got married, you know." On and on the gossip goes. I listen carefully while pretending not to.

The sun is shining right down on us when we pull into Granddaddy Jim's driveway. He meets us at the door. He holds Mama in his arms while I stand staring at the amazing sight in front of me. My mouth hangs open, and my green eyes, so like Daddy's, stare at the shiny wood floors topped with deep wool rugs. I see shiny glass lamps, that I later learn are called crystal chandeliers, that magically light up the whole place when Granddaddy Jim pushes a button on the wall. The kitchen is filled with marble counters, shiny wood cabinets, and a big, gleaming green and black cookstove.

A red pump on the edge of the sink pumps water into a deep marble sink. From the living room a winding staircase leads us up to an actual bathroom. It has a wondrous claw-foot bathtub with gold faucets, a white deep sink with the same gold faucets, and a white toilet stool.

Wow, Mama lived in this house? My mama? Wow! The thought that Mama had another life before us is as thrilling as it is unsettling.

The walls in this house are covered with pictures of Mama and her brothers and sisters. One painting of Mama shows her to be a girl about my age with long, glossy, ringlet curls that float down over her shoulders. Her smile is as bright as the beacon in a lighthouse. She is dressed in a white, ruffled, floaty dress with pink rosebuds on the belt.

Why don't I look like this? And why can't I have a dress like this?

Another picture shows her to be older. Her beautiful dark hair is short, her shiny dress barely covers her knees, her beautiful smile holds a secret only she knows, and her hooded eyes look mysteriously at something.

I will never be this beautiful, I think hopelessly as I glance in the mirror close by at my freckled face, my big nose that runs all the time because of allergies, scraggly reddish hair, and my huge English ears. My scrawny body is wearing a rainbow-striped dress made out of a flour sack.

Later when she is tucking me into bed I ask, "Mama, am I pretty?"

"It's not how you look on the outside, it's how you look on the inside that makes you pretty," she says. I hear from her what I always hear from Ted—"You're egg-sucking ugly."

What is egg-sucking anyway? It must be pretty bad.

40

As soon as I can I sneak around, my eyes wide in wonder as I look into all five of the upstairs bedrooms that run along a narrow hallway. Each has plum-colored velvet drapes and fluffy white curtains over the long narrow windows. I run my fingers over the fancy carved walnut headboards on beds covered with colorful quilts and mounds of satin pillows.

In the next room I check the white iron bedsteads for leftover gum. At home we plaster our gum on our headboards when we go to sleep at night to make it last for a week.

Granddaddy Jim's bedroom is downstairs. I sneak in to see a headboard with the name Benson carved in fancy writing right in the middle of it. A big painting of my Grandmother Carrie is above it. Mama told me she died before I was born. The whole house smells faintly of Granddaddy Jim's special apple pipe tobacco and his Old Spice shaving lotion.

In the living room is a huge brown leather couch and a matching leather chair. No one but Granddaddy Jim sits in his chair, but I crawl up in his lap every chance I get. He holds me quietly while he puffs on his pipe. When I look in his steely blue eyes, I can tell he sees far off things.

I love my Granddaddy Jim so much my heart hurts. This house must be what heaven is like. When I sit on Granddaddy Jim's lap, I can see out his big bay window. "It's not too pretty now," he says of the bushes without leaves, "but soon they will sprout lilacs and yellow roses." From his chair we can see everyone who goes by his house.

One day Aunt Helen comes to the house and sees me sitting on Granddaddy Jim's lap. She jerks me off, and plops her own baby down, and says, in a shrieking voice, "You're too big to be sitting on him, get in the other room. Go help your mother. Find something else to do."

Granddaddy Jim says nothing, just lets her do it.

Maybe she's right. Maybe I am too big to be sitting on Granddaddy. After all, I'm almost seven. I am red with shame as I stumble over his footstool. Confused, I wonder, *Why does she hate me?* I feel as needy as a flower without water.

After that it seems like Aunt Helen is always there— her big-boned body towers over me, telling me I look like a "street urchin."

"Good night, nurse," she says, "you're six years old and you can't even tie your shoes, and pull up your socks. Look at the way they scrunch into your heels. Even Charlene knows enough to pull up her socks."

Her daughter with her dark curly hair and big innocent eyes, is only four years old and is expected to be perfect. Aunt Helen harshly scolds her if she doesn't act like a lady or won't eat what's put in front of her.

I feel sorry for Charlene as Aunt Helen makes her eat everything on her plate. One night she tries to force me to eat rice which I gag on, until Daddy says, "That's alright honey, you don't have to eat that." Silently gloating at Aunt Helen, I leave the room. *My daddy saved me. I know Aunt Helen doesn't like him either. Why is she so mean?*

I try to remember to keep my shoes tied and my socks pulled up, so Aunt Helen will leave me alone. My shoes are making my feet hurt. When I show Mama that my shoes are too small, she gives me an old brown pair of Ted's high-top shoes and makes me try them on.

"I can't wear these ugly brown shoes. They're boy's shoes."

"Put them on and just be glad you have shoes. There's a war going on! Some kids don't even have shoes. You can make this sacrifice."

That makes as much sense to me as when she says, "Eat your supper, there are children in Germany starving."

Huh? How does wearing Ted's old brown shoes help kids who don't have shoes? And how can eating the food on my plate stop children in Germany from starving? I will never understand grown-ups!

In school the next day I try to be invisible. I am the new girl and only one girl is even nice to me. *Maybe if I don't talk to anybody, they won't notice my shoes. I just won't get out of my desk not even to go to the bathroom.*

"Look at her, na-na-na-na. She's wearing boy's shoes." Some of the girls circle around me after school and make jokes about my ugly shoes.

At home I say, "Mama all the kids are laughing at me because of my shoes."

"Don't mind them, just rise above it."

Easy for you to say, you don't know what it's like.

"What you have to do," Ted says, "is learn to fight —
like this." He jabs me in the shoulder with his fists and
in minutes we are rolling on the floor wrestling. "Boys
don't hit girls," Daddy says, pulling Ted up by the
collar.

What? Where have you been all the other times he did?

To me he says, "Hold your head high and be proud.
You're a Jones. Don't let them see that it bothers you. Let
God take care of them."

In my mind I think, *God doesn't give a damn about me.
Oops, I better not ever say that word out loud!*

The teasing is worse the next day. The day after that I
can't get my head to lift very high because my eyes want
to fix themselves on the ground.

§

One morning in April, the sun shining brightly in my
window wakes me up early. Sleepily rubbing the sand
out of my eyes, I wobble to Mama's bedroom. The bed is
empty, the quilt undisturbed, and the bathroom is
empty too. I run downstairs to a cold and silent kitchen.
This doesn't feel right. *Something is very wrong. Where are
Mama and Daddy?* Wide awake now, I run upstairs again
and see the boys peacefully sleeping in their beds. Back
downstairs, I stand outside Granddaddy Jim's bedroom,
but I don't dare go in.

I curl up on the couch in my flannel pajamas, suck
my thumb and wrestle with my worried thoughts. *What
should I do? Should I wake up Ted? He doesn't like me to*

wake him up when he's sleeping. Would he yell at me? Will he tell me how dumb I am?

Finally, I hear my daddy walk in the backdoor and I race to meet him, throwing my arms around his waist. "Where were you?"

"You have a new baby brother," Daddy says, real proud like. "He's a real champion." The look on Daddy's face tells me he is pleased as punch, whatever that is. "Go wake up the boys," he says, "You gotta get ready for school."

"Come on guys, wake up, we have a new brother." My voice is steady now that Daddy is home. I'm no longer afraid but in charge. While Daddy is cooking oatmeal, he jerks open a kitchen drawer and hands me a red crayon. "Put a big X on the calendar to mark this day," he says. It is April 16, 1945.

Granddaddy Jim pads into the kitchen in his furry slippers. "How's Edith?" he asks.

"She had a rough night but she's going to be all right," Daddy replies.

Why did Mama have a rough night? Why does she have to go to the hospital? Is it to pick out just the right baby? The last time I asked her where babies come from, she said, "God sends them." I wonder how He does that.

Ted and I pepper Daddy with questions while we eat our oatmeal.

"When's Mama coming home with the baby?"

"What's his name?"

"What does he look like?"

"His name's Bernie and he looks like a baby."

Daddy must not have looked close enough at the baby or he would know what he looks like.

"Mama will be in the hospital for a few days. When she comes home, I expect all of you to help her and be really good kids, because she's had a hard time."

The week drags on forever. Finally, it's Saturday morning. Daddy goes to pick up Mama while we wait at home all excited. Mama walks in the door helped by Daddy who is holding an armful of sleeping sweetness. A perfect little round face peeks out of the blanket. Daddy hands the bundle to me.

When I breathe the pure, sweet, baby scent of oil and powder along with a whiff of Daddy's Aqua Velva shaving lotion, it is instant love. From that day on, Bernie is my baby. I dress him, feed him, and run home from school to play with him like a doll.

§

Just before school ends for the year, Mrs. Peterson, our music teacher, a round, plump, gray-haired, old woman of at least forty, asks my class if any girls would like to sing in the Memorial Day program. One by one girls raise a hand. *Do I dare volunteer? Can I even sing? I always sing in Sunday school, so maybe I can.* To my surprise my hand shoots up of its own accord.

I race to Granddaddy Jim's house, and tell Mama, "I'm going to be in a program. I'm going to sing."

"Oh," she says. Mama does not understand that the only reason I want to sing is to be like her. I love to hear the beautiful soprano solos that she sings in church every Sunday. I'm so proud that people call on her to sing at funerals and weddings. *I want to be like Mama.*

Staying after school every day I sing my heart out as I learn the words to *America the Beautiful, Faith of Our Fathers*, and *The White Cliffs of Dover.*

I also make a couple of new friends and I don't feel so left out anymore. When Mrs. Peterson puts me in the front row I feel as important as Shirley Temple for being part of something this big. Mrs. Peterson says Memorial Day is the most important day of the year and is about being a proud American.

"Girls," she says one day, "tell your mother you need to wear a white dress and tie some red and blue ribbons in your hair."

"Mama," I say, all excited, "we have to wear white dresses and put blue and red bows in our hair."

"I don't have time to make you a white dress, you're going to have to wear your pink one."

Nooo! You can't make me do that. I will die. My heart sinks to the floor. Mama always means what she says.

"I'm in the front row. I'll be the only girl there without a white dress. I can't stand up there in my old pink dress. Everybody will laugh at me." I knew I'd lose my new friends for sure.

My whining doesn't help. "You'll be just fine. I'm sure there will be others there without a white dress." Mama's voice is firm.

At the next practice I can't sing for thinking horrifying thoughts of pink dresses, boy's shoes and how the other kids will tease me. *Maybe I will run away. I wonder if Mama will miss me. I know, I will just play sick.*

On the Saturday before the Monday program, I am moping around the house when mama's cousin Evelyn shows up. "How's my favorite namesake?" she asks. Evelyn is so pretty and doesn't let things bother her. She's what Mama call's "elegant" as her high heels click across the wooden floor. She owns her own band-uniform factory in a faraway place called Minneapolis. She often sends me gifts, usually scarves or mittens.

I hang my head and talk low so Mama won't hear. "I'm in the program, right in the front row. I've learned all the songs and I need a white dress and Mama won't get me one, and I have to wear those old brown shoes."

"Oh Edith, this girl's got to have a white dress," Evelyn tells my mother. She goes to her suitcase and takes a white dress out, rips it up, and sits down at Mama's sewing machine. All day she works on the dress.

"Stay right here. Don't you go anywhere now. I need you to try this on," she tells me.

I love Aunt Evelyn. She is my hero. *Now I don't have to play sick or run away or kill myself. I wish she could be my mother. Oh God, something terrible is going to happen to me for such an awful thought.*

Finally, Evelyn hands me a perfect white dress with puffed sleeves and a full skirt. Throwing my arms around her I say, "Thank you, thank you, thank you!"

"You're welcome, sweetheart. Just consider this your birthday present."

I forgot I'm going to be seven years old in two days.

On Memorial Day I walk proudly on stage in my new white dress, and new white shoes (another birthday present, Daddy said). I am dressed like the other nineteen girls. We are a sea of white with pink faces, and shining hair tied with red and blue ribbons. Our hands are folded neatly in front of our bodies and all of us are singing at the top of our lungs. I am the proudest of all, knowing I've just escaped a fate worse than death.

§

My birthday gets lost in the buzz of overhearing Mama and Daddy say we are moving to a farm outside of town. They hardly ever tell us anything. We find out things from sneaking and listening.

Ted is excited. He jumps up and down saying, "We get to have horses and cows!"

"Mama," I ask as sadness punches me in the stomach, "Why do we have to leave Granddaddy Jim's house?"

"Because," Mama says, "he's going to sell this house and move in with his sister."

"Why? I don't want to leave this house. Why can't we buy it?"

"Stop being so selfish. We'll have a whole farm to live on, and we're going to love it."

"Granddaddy Jim," I say, leaning against him and wrapping my arms around him, "I don't want to leave you."

In his calm, gracious way, he pats me on the head and says, "I'm giving you a piano."

My heart lights up like a thousand candles. *A piano, really? My own piano? How does he know I want to take piano lessons? I'm going to have my own piano!*

"Mama, Mama!" My feet barely touch the ground as I run around the house searching for her. When I find her, I yell, "Granddaddy Jim gave me a piano! Now I can take piano lessons."

Mama's response is a dagger in my chest. "No, you wouldn't keep at it and we'd have to drive four miles for lessons. Besides, I donated the piano to the church."

Mama gave my piano away!

§

The farmhouse has been here for a hundred years, Ted tells me. It's been sitting empty for a while, and it rattles, creaks, and groans. Hot wind blows in through the drafty windows. *Are there ghosts in here?*

Everybody else is keen on the idea of living on a farm. *Why can't I be excited like the other kids? I have a strange bad feeling about it that grabs me. Some bad things are going to happen here, I can just feel it.* I try to tell Mama what I feel, but she is busy. *No point talking to her.*

"Ted, it feels strange here."

"No, it doesn't. We are going to have a horse. Granddaddy Jim is giving us a horse."

The boys claim the big upstairs room and I get the small narrow one with a walk-in closet. Somebody painted it blue and white and Mama made flowy white curtains that hang starched and ironed at the tall window. My old dresser sits across the room with its scratches from being moved so much and the big round mirror at the top. Two apple crates with a curtain on a spring stretched between them, and a painted board on top are what Mama calls a vanity. *My own room, my own vanity, my own dresser! Not as nice as Granddaddy Jim's house but not bad.*

Mama and my favorite aunt, Dorothy, who is married to Mama's brother Bud, slap up white wallpaper with pink roses in the square living room, paste some oil paper on the kitchen walls, and smooth it with clean rags tied to a broom.

Daddy's painting the woodwork. I watch as he puts some stinky glue on the rough wood floors and rolls out shiny red linoleum from wall to wall. He looks so handsome with his sleeves rolled up, his dark hair hanging in his sweaty face, and his muscles popping from his shirt sleeves. I can't resist throwing my arms around his neck as he kneels on the floor. He grins at me and says, "Gotta work fast, honey, before the glue dries. Go check out the cellar and bring up some of the bricks for me so I can set them on the floor to keep the linoleum down."

A narrow white door in the middle of the short hallway takes me to a stairway that leads to the cellar where we can keep coal, canned goods, onions, and potatoes.

Mama is so excited the day the men from Montgomery Ward deliver the new iron cookstove. It has two ovens, four round black grates on top with a fancy silver wire handle to lift each grate out, making it easier to drop in coal or wood. A deep well called a water reservoir covers one whole side of the big black stove. The reservoir means we'll always have hot water. Daddy fires the stove up and Mama puts a pewter tea kettle on it. When it's hot It whistles. The tin coffee pot is always on as well.

The saggy dirt floor garage is a few feet from the house. Ted has fun climbing on the rafters in the garage even though they are full of bird poop and bat's nests— until Daddy catches him. "You will fall and break your arm, or worse your legs."

"But, Dad, look what I've found." Ted shows off old buffalo robe and a horse whip hidden on a board laid across the rafters. Mama says somebody used the buffalo robe to keep warm when driving to town with a team and buggy. The horse whip provides hours of fun as we pretend to be cowboys or pirates, master and slave. I feel so strong when we crack the whip.

The farm also has old tin granaries, a fallen down wooden chicken coop, and a long gray hog house that sure does stink. There are also washed-out-looking wooden wagons and hayracks in the barnyard, plus all kinds of iron machinery that can be pulled by horses. A faded red barn full of stalls, smells of horse manure and hay.

Wonder of wonders in the first stall is old Bird, the beautiful reddish-brown horse with the stark white blaze across her face, that Granddaddy Jim says is all ours. A few old saddles and bridles hang by the big double doors that are swung open. Daddy says the doors will need a lot of repair before they will ever close again.

In the middle of the barn is a ladder on the wall leading to a haymow. We climb the ladder and pull ourselves up through the hole in the ceiling to the center of the haymow. Under some loose hay, we find an old trunk, some old picture frames and some strange black and white pictures on metal that Mama calls tintypes. The haymow is a great place to play even if it is full of dust and rustles with mice moving around, and bats and birds flying.

"Boy is this old," Daddy says about a funny looking saddle with a tiny seat that he calls an army saddle.

Ted wastes no time learning how to put a saddle and bridle on Bird.

"Let me try. Let me try," I say.

"Nah, you're a girl," Ted spits out.

But Daddy walks by and says, "Ted, teach your sister how to put a saddle and a bridle on a horse."

Bird stands still while we curry her mane and tail, and rub her down. She's patient as I practically maul her to death when I hug her. To get on her back, I have to climb up on a pile of tires. Mostly she holds steady while we put on her saddle and bridle, but sometimes she clamps her teeth shut and refuses to take the bit. Ted can usually sweet-talk her into opening her mouth. She strolls around the barnyard with three or four of us on her back. But we have to watch out as she likes to wander over to the clothesline and go under it to scrape us off. I swear she's laughing while we dust ourselves off.

§

The outhouse looks like it's falling apart. The paint is worn off, but it has three holes on a splintery board. At least this outhouse has a hole small enough to fit my butt.

I want Granddaddy Jim's nice clean bathroom. I miss him and wish we could go live in his house. Daddy gets mad at me if I say this out loud, so I can't tell anybody how bad I feel. *Nobody cares anyway.*

Every morning, I get up and stumble, half asleep, to the little wooden building with the old Sears catalogue and newspapers lying on the dusty floor that we use for toilet paper. The secret is to avoid the shiny pages, take a black-and-white page from the catalogue, crumble it between your hands, roll it around and around, and squish it until it is softer before wiping with it.

Sometimes early in the morning I don't bother to go all the way to the outhouse, I just squat out of sight at the corner of the house. The outhouse stinks so much when it's hot in the summer that I hold my breath as long as I can to avoid the slimy stink, while the flies swarm buzzing around my head. A sticky fly-strip hangs from the ceiling, and I hear the insects making angry buzzing sounds as they try to free themselves from the tacky glue that holds them captive until they die. Mama throws away the fly-strip when it gets full and puts another one up. There is one small window above the bench of holes but it doesn't let in much light because it is covered in dust and flies caught in spider webs.

In the winter when the weather is really bad and there are piles of ice and snow around the outhouse, we use chamber pots and slop pails with lids. They are placed in the cold spare room upstairs. It is freezing in that room, but at least we don't have to go outside. Every day Daddy trudges up the stairs and tromps back down with the stinky buckets. He empties them in the fields, washes them out at the icy well, and brings them back in. I feel bad for him when I see him walk to the back door with a bucket in each hand.

There is no electricity in our house and Daddy swears about something called the REA, that he says is "moving toward our house like a snail with a hundred pounds on its back." We use an Aladdin lantern filled with gas and we also use candles and kerosene lamps. All the lamps have wicks that need to be trimmed before every use and the glass chimneys fill up with soot and smoke, and we have to keep them clean. Mike and I clean the thin glass chimneys every day. Mike and I also polish the silverware once a week, rubbing the shiny silver until it glistens like a diamond in the sun.

We aren't allowed to carry the lamps or the candles because we might set the house on fire. At night, Mama and Daddy carry kerosene lamps with their dim, yellow glow from room to room. If we want to go upstairs for something, we better do it before it gets dark. Sometimes we beg Mama to light the way for us.

Chapter Five

Life on the Farm

Groggy as I wake from a sound sleep, I hear Daddy's voice carry up the stairs through the dark. He's yelling at Mama. *This isn't right. What's wrong?*

"Just because your daddy is rich doesn't mean the bastard can tell us how to live."

"Lon, you've been drinking. Shush, you'll wake the kids."

"They should know what a son of a bitch he is. He stole this farm."

"Lon, please keep your voice down. He didn't steal this farm."

"He damn sure did."

Their voices dip and spurt. The louder my daddy gets, the softer my mother speaks until I can't hear her at all.

"Your goddamn father and your goddamn brothers think I'm a piece of shit."

I fall asleep to the voices and the next morning I wonder if I really heard what I heard. I feel cockamamie dizzy. I've heard Ted use those words and they seem to fit.

As I lug a heavy pail of water to the house from the well, I think about what Daddy said about Granddaddy Jim stealing this farm. I can't stop thinking about it. *How could Grandad do that?* I wonder as I push the big iron pump handle up and down, up and down, up and down. When there is no wind, we have to pump our water.

The first time I tried to pump water, Ted and I had to put all our weight on the pump handle to force the water out. I can do it by myself now. We even have contests to see who can pump a pail of water fastest. Ted hates it if I beat him. He was so mad one time that he threw a pail of water at me.

The windmill is a great place to play and we climb the ladder every chance we get. When my mother catches us, she yells. Furious, she stands at the bottom of the tower of tin that rises above the flat countryside, screaming at the top of her lungs and waving her arms. "You kids get off that windmill. You could kill yourselves—break your arms." Ted is already at the top, and I am close behind him. Mike is half-way up, and Bill is climbing slowly behind us.

"Don't you know how dangerous this is?" she says when we reach the ground. Her hair is standing on end from the wind and her face is red.

Pools of water sit at the base of the well when it rains, bringing out garter snakes and all kinds of frogs and tadpoles. We like to wait and watch the snakes swallow the tadpoles, then we smack the snake right in the middle of its belly with the side of our hands and watch the tadpole bounce back out. Once we fed the tadpole back to the snake several times, so everyone could have a turn.

Even though our old farmhouse is shabby and nothing at all like Granddaddy Jim's fancy house, old Bird makes up for the difference. I soon find out there is nothing like the wind in my hair and the air rushing past my cheeks on warm summer days as I fly over a field on old Bird.

I race her into the barnyard when Daddy stands beside the barn watching. "You can't let this horse get this hot. She's twenty years old. You should know better."

How would I know better? Nobody told me that. Whenever Daddy or Mama get mad at me they say I should know better.

Daddy yells at Ted who is cleaning out Bird's stall. "Come get this horse. Rub her down and cool her off."

Ted glares at me.

"You," Daddy says, pointing his finger in my face, "get in the house and help your mother."

I hate it when Daddy is cross with me. "I didn't even know I was doing anything wrong," I mutter on the way to the house.

§

Monday is washday, and hauling water from the well is a lot of work. Early in the morning Daddy hustles in pail after pail of water and pours it in a big copper boiler to heat water to wash the clothes. My job is to take the stinky diapers that have been sitting in a pail on the porch out to the well, pump icy water into the pail, and rinse out the smelly brown crap in the diapers, one by one. I hold my breath as much as I can.

I dip the stinky diapers up and down, up and down, and squeeze the brownish water out with my frozen red hands, and lay the diapers on a rock by the well. I empty the bucket in the barnyard, throw the diapers back into the pail and take them to where Mama is waiting on the porch with the wringer washer and rinse tubs all set up.

The baby clothes go in first, with one-quarter cup of blueing, to keep them from getting yellow. Then the other whites. Overalls and black things go in last. If I don't have to run off to school, I help hang everything on the clothesline wearing a clothespin bag around my waist. In the summer I like doing it, but in the winter my hands freeze and so do the clothes.

Daddy brings in lots of water on Saturday nights for our once-a-week bath. He fills the round tin tub, sets it on top of the iron stove to heat water for our baths. When the water is warm enough, he lifts the tub to the floor in the kitchen and it's bath time—babies first, then us kids, stair-step up by age. That puts me somewhere in the middle. Then Ted, and finally Mama.

We have an enamel sink that sits under the high kitchen window. On one end of the sink is a bucket with a tin dipper for drinking water. We all drink out of the same dipper. Inside the double tin doors under the sink are two pails. One is to catch the water dumped from the dipper, or spills from the red enamel dishpan. Dishwater or handwashing water is carried to the back door and flung into the yard. The other pail is for food scraps to feed the pigs.

Somebody has to empty those stinky five-gallon pails, usually Daddy or Ted. In a pinch I can take one side and Mama the other, and we limp it out to the barnyard. A blue enamel pan for handwashing sits in the hollow porcelain sink that has small holes where faucets should be. Every time I look at those holes, I think about Granddaddy Jim's gold faucets. The towel for drying hands hangs on a rack nearby. It's grimy by the end of each day.

Something Granddaddy Jim doesn't have, and that we've never had before, is the brown wooden telephone box on the wall in a corner of the kitchen. It has a mouthpiece that sticks out from the center and a cone-shaped piece that hangs on one side. It's a party line and all six families on it have their very own ring. Ours is four shorts and a long. It doesn't matter whose ring it is, anytime it rings everybody on the line picks up the receiver and listens in. There are no secrets on a party line.

It's suppertime when Mama answers the ringing telephone. "How did it happen? When? Where? What, time?" she asks. When she hangs up the phone, she looks confused and like she doesn't know what to do. She looks at Daddy and says, "Ann's dead. She was killed in a car wreck last night. And Oleta is in the hospital. She was driving the car." We eat in silence as I think about the last time I saw my cousins.

Daddy goes to be with his sister Pearl, the next day and the rest of us stay home to do the chores. I feel so sad, but I don't say anything. I picture my cousin Ann lying dead on the road. *Did she bleed to death? Did she cry? I wonder what it feels like to die?*

I dream about her lying in a ditch and I wake up crying. The outhouse is the only place I can go to be alone so I sit there watching the flies and think, *Did Ann go to heaven or hell?* I hope it is heaven but our minister said everybody will go to hell unless they do certain things. *Did Ann do those certain things?*

§

Sometimes Daddy comes in the house and says, "I need to run into town for some feed." Sometimes he needs a piece of machinery. Then Ted and Mama have to feed the pigs, bring in the cows from the field, and water the horses. Mike and I collect the eggs.

One night Daddy comes home late in the evening when we are all in our pajamas drinking hot cocoa at the table. Mama is telling us a story about when she was a little girl and lived above Granddaddy Jim's hardware store in town.

Daddy comes hustling in the door looking all happy. "Here kids," he says, his eyes shiny, as he reaches in his pockets, grabs all his coins and throws them in the air. "Go get 'em."

We scramble after the money, Ted getting the most. Daddy says to Bill, "Look over here," and to Mike he says, "Check under the table."

Mama is warming up his supper at the woodstove. The dim kerosene lamp barely gives enough light for her to see what she's doing.

"Sit down Lon."

That's funny, Daddy is sort of wobbly. He gets to his chair and starts singing a song we are learning to know by heart, because he sings it a lot.

> *Old Dan Tucker, the damned old man, washed his face in a frying pan.*
>
> *Old Dan Tucker's going to town, wearing his shirt upside down.*
>
> *Old Dan Tucker, the damned old fool, couldn't even ride his mule.*
>
> *Old Dan Tucker combed his hair with a wagon wheel and died with a toothache in his heel.*

"This is how to do a jig," he says as he gets up from his chair and hooks his arm through first mine, and then the other kids' arms, until we were all going around and around in the middle of the floor and we all fell down. Mama then says, "You kids go to bed. School starts tomorrow. Here's your supper Lon."

Daddy is so much fun! Why doesn't Mama want us to have any?

I'm in bed waiting for someone to come hear my prayers. I can hear Mama and Daddy downstairs. Mama sounds mad. Daddy is yelling, "You know it's true." I can't hear Mama's answer.

I hear Daddy again, "Those SOB brothers of yours won't be happy until I'm ruined."

Are Mama's brothers being mean to Daddy? Why?

I hear Daddy plodding up the stairs to hear our prayers. He goes to the boys' room first, then he comes to mine. He picks me up and sets me on his knee. Burying his face in my hair he says, "I'm so glad I have you. You're the only one who loves me." Sleepily, I pat his face, feeling angry at Mama for making Daddy feel bad.

The next morning I feel guilty and strangely superior to Mama.

§

I'm in the second grade. Thanks to Granddaddy Jim, there is a one-room schoolhouse across the road. He built it on his land "especially for his grandchildren," Mama said.

New shoes and coats come in the mail from Sears and Roebuck along with new underwear. I am so excited about school and meeting the six other kids who go there. They have to come a long way and the teacher has to drive four miles. Proudly, I tell my brothers, "Granddaddy Jim built this school just for us."

The look on Mama's face is stormy. "Ladies don't brag or tell all they know."

"Why are you mad at me? It's true."

Now what did I do wrong? I was just telling the truth.

"It's not nice to brag. And I'm not mad. Ladies don't get mad." Mama says.

Chapter Six

What Farm Kids Do

There's no school today because we're having a threshing bee. Farm kids stay home to help on days like this. All the neighbors are here with pitchforks, trucks, and threshing machines. Mrs. Hagenlock and Aunt Dorothy have brought mountains of chicken to fry, piles of hot rolls, pies, cakes and cookies, and jugs full of tea. The kitchen is filled with food and bustling women in housedresses.

"Here Bubbles, peel the potatoes," Aunt Dorothy says. I'd do anything for her but I think this looks like a lot of potatoes, as she sets a gunnysack full of potatoes in front of a spindly kitchen chair and hands me a knife.

Mama is frying chicken. Aunt Dorothy is cutting cabbage for slaw. Mrs. Hagenlock is heaping slabs of cake and piles of cookies on platters. The heat from the stove makes me hot and sweaty. There is no refrigerator and no ice but the tea is set in a tub of icy cold water from the well.

Before the threshers come in to eat, each man goes to the well to splash cold water on his dusty face and dirty hands. They grab the tin cup hanging by the pump and chug down water.

Watching Mama fry chicken over the hot stove, wiping her forehead with her apron, I think about the baby chickens we raised in the spring and how many we killed in the fall.

It was awful. Daddy cut their heads off and then we watched the headless chickens do a dance around the barnyard before they fell over dead. We dipped the dead chickens into pails of boiling hot water, pulled off the stinky feathers, and gutted them, pulling out the heart, gizzard, and liver for frying. Then we threw the soggy feathers and disgusting chicken innards over the back fence as fast as we could. I thought, I'd never be able to eat chicken again, but when it's on the table, it's just too good to pass up.

§

Whir, treadle, whir, treadle, whir treadle, whir, treadle, whir. The low noise of the treadle sewing machine can put me to sleep. Mama is making me a new dress for Thanksgiving. I watch her and listen as she sings, her beautiful soprano voice filling the living room.

I am trying to entertain Bernie so he won't bother her.

"Here go try this dress on and see if it fits—and be careful of the pins." Mama hands me a green corduroy dress with a pinned in Peter Pan collar. Her hands flick quickly across my back fitting it to my body.

Why can't she just hug me?

But commands are already on her lips. "Go see what the boys are up to. And set the table before Dad comes in so he'll think supper is almost ready."

Mama comes upstairs every night to tuck us into bed, and listen while we say our prayers. She kisses me on the forehead before she goes to tuck the boys in. I do my best to fall asleep, turning first one way and then another, but my eyes are wide open, staring into the dark. I'm so scared of the monsters in the closet that only come out after everyone is asleep but me.

§

It's June, I celebrate my eighth birthday in the snow this year. Seven girls including two of my cousins come to help me celebrate and eat birthday cake. As I open one package after another, I see anklets, pink, blue, white, green, underpants with the days of the week embroidered on them, some doll clothes that Mama made for my favorite doll, and some colored pencils.

I feel disappointed, but what do I expect?

Aunt Pearl comes to visit us a few days after my birthday and brings my cousin Bobbie, who is Ted's age, and six-year old Larry, a loud, skinny scrap of a kid with dishwater blond hair and freckles on his nose. There is nothing Larry won't try—he even chases the goats in the barnyard. Larry, Mike, and I are playing in the yard.

Larry says in a voice that sounds like he knows a secret. "I've learned a new word." He always knows stuff we don't.

"Tell us the word."

"Nah, You wouldn't get it."

"Yes we will. Pleeaasse."

69

"Okay. It's *fuck*."

"I heard my daddy say that in the kitchen the other night. What's it mean?"

"Well, I think it means you take off all your clothes and pee on each other. Want ta see what I mean? Come on." He runs for the outhouse. We peel off all our clothes and stand stupidly looking at each other's private parts. I couldn't pee on their legs and I sure wasn't going to let them pee on mine.

"Suck on this," Larry says, holding out his penis toward me.

So I did. It rolled around like a warm earthworm for maybe a minute and it was gross. "Yuck, let's go play ball," I say.

We pulled our clothes back on and I hear Mama calling me. "Come in and set the table. Daddy's going to be coming in from cutting alfalfa."

He must be comin' in early because Aunt Pearl is here. What would Mama say if she knew what we been doin'?

Daddy farms with two teams of horses. Sometimes he uses Mabel and Diamond and other times he uses Sam and Fannie. When he's pulling the manure spreader he hooks all four of them up at once. I watch him put the harnesses on the fat old pluggers, talking to them like he talks to people. "Stand still now," he says. "That's a good girl. That's a good boy." He seems to have lots of patience with the horses, calming and soothing them when they stomp and throw their heads at flies.

70

But why does my sweet and gentle Daddy get so mad after he's been to town? But he never says bad things about Mama after he comes home. He just talks about how unfair his life is, and what assholes other people are, and doesn't she know how her brothers use and abuse him? Doesn't he help them every damn time they ask, and do they ever lift a finger to help him? And doesn't he loan them his tools and machinery and never get it back? Mama always listens patiently.

Poor Daddy, why is everybody so mean to him?

One morning I'm watching him with the horses.

He asks, "What are you doing up so early?"

"I can't sleep. Daddy, why do you have to do this?"

"Because we have to eat." He grabs the horses' reins and clucks at them as they pull him and a plow out of the barnyard through the big iron gate toward the pasture.

Later, as she often does in the summer, Mama sends Ted, Mike, and me out to the field to bring Daddy lunch. Our bare feet sink in the dirt and we hop over thistles as we stumble over plowed furrows and stubble. We take turns carrying a stuffed paper bag filled with sandwiches and cookies wrapped in wax paper and a heavy stone water jug with fresh, icy well water. When Daddy sees us coming, he pulls the team over and waters the horses from canvas water bags, fastens the reins to a handle on the plow, and waits for us to get there. I watch him gulp the jug of water and peel back the wax paper from the thick beef sandwiches. I'm happy to be out in the sun and fresh air on fields that go as far as I can see.

When Daddy gets to the cookies he always says, "Here, you kids better eat these." His sparkling blue-green eyes, peek out from a curtain of dust, and his dry peeling lips look red against the powder of dirt covering his cheeks. He pours a little water from the horse's water bag on his red bandana and wipes his face, leaving streaks of dirt on his sunburned skin. He bangs his straw hat against his knee and puffs of dust fly out around us. As he gets back on the seat of the plow, we walk away swinging an empty jug. A feeling of love for Daddy rises up in me like the air bubbles that float to the top of the water tank after a strong wind forces the water to gush from the well.

Going back home we stop in the cool grove of cottonwood and elm trees just north of our house. Among the moss, grass, and weeds, we search for sheep sorrel so we can put it in our mouths and chew it. I love the sweet-sour taste. The trees are filled with birds and provide us with lots of wood to split for the woodstove. In the spring, we rescue baby birds that fall from their nests. In the grove are a couple of old cars that we use for pirate ships, or castles, depending on our mood.

Ted and I catch crows because Ted says they can learn to talk. We do our best to make one talk but that never happens. "You gotta slit their tongue," Daddy says when we tell him what we are doing. We try but we can never hold a crow still long enough to find its tongue.

While Daddy is working day and night in the fields, Mama does women's work. Daddy tells us what's men's work and what's women's work.

"My women don't work in the barn or the field like some common hired hand."

When I ask to learn how to milk the cows, or when I wonder why the boys get to go with him in the wagon but I don't, he says, "You need to be a lady like your mother and act ladylike. Your mother is a soft, gentle, beautiful lady, and I want you to be just like her."

Maybe he doesn't know what my tummy already knows—there is only room for one lady in this house. Besides I don't want to be like Mama. Her work—scrubbing floors and walls, sitting at a sewing machine, washing clothes and dishes—is boring and has to be done over and over.

"Women's work never gets done," I tell Mama. "When I grow up, I'm going to have a job and pay someone to do the housework and wash the clothes."

She laughs at me, "You silly girl, there are no jobs for women unless you want to be a teacher or a hired girl. You're going to get married and have a houseful of kids, so you'd better learn how to do these things. Anyway, it's an honor to be a woman. Just be glad you're not a man; they have to do the really hard work."

I've been begging Daddy to let me learn to milk the cows. "Please, Daddy, I can do it. I can probably even do it better than Ted. Please Daddy?"

Finally he says, "Okay. Damnit, Ted, teach your sister how to milk old Bessie."

"What ya wanta do that for?" Ted asks me.

"Because it looks like fun and I hate housework."

The barn is dark, cool, and smelly. The milking has to be done while it is still light out because everybody knows the horror stories about barns that burn down if you take a lantern in there and it gets tipped over.

Handing me a three-legged stool and using his best big-brother voice, Ted says, "You put the stool beside Bessie and sit on it like this." He shows me how to spread my legs apart, turning the three-legged stool into a five legged stool. "Lean your head into the cow's side, like this."

Bessie stands still while I practice putting my head against her flank. She swats me with her manure-tipped tail a few times while I grab the teats the way Ted shows me and squeeze. When I finally see a thin stream of milk and hear it plunking into the tin milk pail, I am so doggone proud of myself.

"Now," Ted says, "take your thumb and forefinger, start at the top of the teat and strip it, pulling slowly until you get every last drop of milk. If you don't do it right, you'll ruin the cow."

I struggle until I get it right. While I'm struggling, Ted milks the other six cows. He comes to check on me between each cow. Finally, he says, "Hey, Bubs, you did a good job." This bit of praise from my big brother is thrilling.

§

One morning Ted throws a pillowcase over my head and holds it tightly around my throat while I scream, kick, and wave my arms, barely getting out a muffled, "I can't breathe!" When I go limp, he lets me up.

I look everywhere for Daddy so I can tell him what Ted did to me. He isn't in the barn, not in the garage, not in the outhouse, not feeding the pigs, or the chickens. "Mama, I can't find Daddy." I hope Daddy will tell Ted, "You better be nice to your sister; she's the only one you *got.*"

Mama answers, "He went to town a while ago to get some feed; he'll be back for supper." Supper comes; no Daddy. We wait, food keeping warm on the stove, and then we wait some more. "I guess we better eat," Mama finally says. It's dark now.

The door opens and we see Daddy's old dirty, cream-colored straw hat come sliding across the red tiles of the kitchen floor.

What is he doing?

Daddy follows the hat in, laughing.

"Why'd you do that?" I ask.

"Well, they say if you're not sure you're welcome, you throw your hat in the door. If it gets kicked back out, you leave, and if it stays, you come in."

Mama doesn't think it's funny. I think it's funny. I throw my arms around his neck and an old beer smell fills up my nose.

"It's time for bed, kids. Get your pajamas on. Bubbles help Bernie get on his pjs."

I'm lying in bed listening to Mama and Daddy. Mama's voice is soft, Daddy's is getting louder and louder, and he's cussing about something. The awful words make my ears hurt.

Is Mama mad at him?

Chapter Seven

Summertime

Daddy hires Kenny and Daphne, who just got married, to work for us as hired hands for the summer. Daphne is a scrap of a woman with a peaked little face and bright red hair. She helps Mama do mama things and Mama gives her some old housedresses to wear. Kenny is a slim, blond guy, with an injured leg. He just got home from fighting in the war. His muscles bulge from his sleeveless shirt, and he is handsome in his dirty, floppy straw hat. Kenny helps Daddy in the field.

"Tell us what it's like in Germany," Ted begs at supper the first night they are here.

"You don't want to know." Kenny shudders as he says this.

Why don't we want to know?

"Shut up and eat," Daddy orders as he points in Ted's direction with his fork.

One evening I walk up the stairs to their room. It's always hot, stuffy, and smoky up there, even with the window open.

"Come on in," Kenny says when I knock on the door. When I go in, he is rolling a cigarette and asks me, "Want ta learn how to roll one?"

They're paying attention to me. They must like me. Besides, it's a challenge. I say yes.

"Like this." Kenny takes the cigarette paper and holds it just so between his thumb and two fingers. With the other hand and his teeth he opens a small, dirty, white cloth bag with yellow drawstrings, and holds the cigarette paper in his left hand while he pours the tobacco into the thin paper. He holds the yellow string with his teeth and pulls the bag shut, carefully licks one side of the paper, and then rolls the whole mess into a fat cigarette that he sticks in his mouth. Lighting it by striking a farmer's match along the rough wood floor, he takes a big suck on it. Then he hands it to Daphne, who takes a big drag, and then hands it to me.

I try it and start choking as tears run down my cheeks. They both laugh and say, "You'll get used to it."

Kenny hands me the papers and tobacco. "Now you try rolling it." At first, I spill tobacco in my lap.

"Be careful," Daphne says, running to get a magazine. "Here, stand up and brush it off on this so we can save it." It takes a couple dozen tries before I can do it without spilling a bunch, but I learn to balance the thin cigarette paper between my thumb and middle finger. Making a dent in it with my forefinger, I pour in the right amount of tobacco and pull the string shut on the pouch with my teeth, just the way Kenny does.

When I smoke, I gag, sputter, and choke over and over, while Kenny and Daphne laugh.

Mama and Daddy would be fighting mad if they knew what I am doing.

§

It's summer, time to go to Bible school. I hope this summer will be different than last.

Either Mama or Daddy drops us off at the church in the morning and then one of them picks us up at noon. About an hour before lunch, I start worrying and hoping it will be Mama because when Daddy comes we always stop downtown in front of the bar.

"I'll be right out, kids," he says. We sit in the car in the sun—hungry, hot, thirsty, and alone. Bored and angry, I wait, and wait, and wait, before marching into the bar. "Daddy, it's time to go home. We're hungry and hot."

Daddy yells at the woman behind the bar, "Bring me four bottles of orange pop and four bags of potato chips." He loads me down with the loot. "Go back to the car. I'll be there soon."

I try to keep Bill and Mike happy, playing games, and singing songs while another hour or two goes by. Ted is off somewhere but he comes back every once in a while, to see if we are leaving yet.

The kids we were with in Bible school this morning come downtown and see us sitting in the car. My face is hot with shame when one asks, "Haven't you gone home yet?"

When I can't take it anymore, I march back into the dark, cool bar to see what is taking Daddy so long. Daddy signals for the bartender to give me more pop and more potato chips. His eyes are flashing and his face is flushed. "Get back to the car. I'll be right out."

I'm mad. *I'm calling mama.* In Charan's General Store I politely ask, "Can I use your phone? I need to call my Mama. "Mama," I plead, "please call the bar and tell Daddy to come home. Please. I want to come home."

"No, I'm not doing that. Just go back to the car and wait. Or, if you want to, you can walk home."

"Mama, please!"

"There is nothing I can do about it."

Is she crazy? Mike and Bill can't walk four miles. I hate Mama and Daddy both. Walking around with Bill in one hand and Mike in the other, I think, *While I'm in the store I might as well help myself.* Quickly, I pick up a nail polish, then a lipstick, and a lotion, and stuff them in my pocket. In the car I admire these treasures. The polish and the lipstick are the most beautiful brilliant red. The lotion smells like roses.

Finally, Daddy comes out. It's almost dark. When we get home Mama isn't there. We yell for her and look upstairs, downstairs, in the cellar, in the outhouse, and in the barn—no Mama. Daddy looks really scared; I can see it in his face.

Then we see Mama way out in the pasture, carrying Bernie. Our old dog Buff is beside her and they're driving the cows in. "The cows were in the oats," she says, "I had to go get them."

"Where is Kenny?"

"Don't you remember he had to take Daphne to the doctor in Faulkton today."

Then the hullabaloo begins. "Bubbles, help Mama. Ted get the milk pails," Daddy barks. Supper's late, but at least it's not potato chips and orange pop.

When Mama comes upstairs to tuck us in for the night, she sees the stuff in my room. Her face tightens up. "Where did you get this?" she asks, holding up the lotion.

"When I got done calling you from Charan's I just walked around and picked it up. No one saw me."

"That's shoplifting! You are taking this back the next time we go into town. Don't you ever do that again." Mama is furious.

Well, it's your fault, I think. *If you'd have picked us up from Bible school I wouldn't have been in the store.* I'm so mad at Mama. She knew he would leave us in the car again and still she let him do it.

At breakfast Daddy yells at me. "You brainless idiot. You called your mother on a party line. How goddamn many people do you think listen in on that party line? What is the matter with you? Don't you know it is nobody's business what goes on in this house? It didn't hurt you to sit in the car. Don't you ever call your mother again."

Ted makes his "you stink" face at me. "Yeah Bubs, that was a really stupid thing to do."

"Oh yeah? Where were you while I was taking care of the little kids?"

"That's your job. You're the maid."

"I am not the maid!" I scream.

"Well you're a girl and that's what girls do."

On Saturday night when I sneak the stolen goods back on the shelf, my knees are knocking. I'm more afraid of getting caught doing the right thing than I'd been of doing the wrong thing.

§

Mama belongs to *Club*. Once a month the farm women, tall, short, fat, skinny—with farmer's tans and scraggly turkey necks, wearing their best housedresses, meet at somebody's house for Club. All afternoon they talk recipes, gardening, kids, and what other people are doing. When they meet at our house I hear them. Their voices get loud or drop low when they are telling something they don't want us to hear.

When it is Mama's turn to have Club, we have to clean the whole inside of our house—scrubbing, waxing, washing windows and curtains, and shoving things in drawers that usually sit out in plain sight. Mike and I polish the silver tea service and the silverware, Mama gets the good china out of boxes in the spare room.

"Why do we have to clean the upstairs? They don't come up here,"

"Just clean it. You never know."

"Why do we have to wash the windows? Why do we have to wash the curtains?"

"Just do it."

On Club day the cut-glass bowls, the thin china with the pink flowers, and the crystal glasses sit on the counter waiting. We lock the dogs and the kittens up in the barn, and clean up any garbage around the path to the door. The smell of cookies and cakes make the house smell so good, but we can't have any until the Club ladies leave.

One Sunday a year, there is a Club picnic. All the daddies and kids are invited to join the fun in the park. We show up with boxes of fried chicken heaped on foil and wax paper, the best vegetables from our gardens piled in brown paper bags, sugar-dripping fruit pies, and cakes with thick chocolate frosting. The daddies carry boxes with Pyrex dishes of food to the wooden picnic tables. The women spread it all out on pretty tablecloths with flowers on them. The daddies sit down at the tables, and kids sit on blankets spread under the trees.

We stuff ourselves full of fried chicken, deviled eggs, potato salad, baked beans, fresh juicy tomatoes, sweet carrots, green onions, homemade bread cut in thick slices, and cucumbers with sour cream.

We can't wait to run out and explore the park while the grown-ups sit and talk. Out of sight, some of the kids start making fun of me for the way I'm dressed. I'm wearing Ted's old jeans and a plaid shirt.

Why won't Daddy let me wear shorts and a mid-rift top like everybody else?

I go back and hang around the picnic table until Mama says, "Go play." Sneaking away from the other kids, I climb a tree and sit up there all afternoon watching them.

"Where did she go? Let's find her and beat her up," one girl says as a few of them walk under the tree I'm hiding in.

I'm happy when Mama calls for me, and I come down from the tree. A couple of the kids help their parents carry food to their cars. "We were looking for you," a girl said in a sweet voice. "We wanted to play with you."

Sure you did, you blood-sucking squirrel.

§

We're sitting in the in the shade by the back door making mud pies. Mike and Bill are making perfect clumps of the brown sticky stuff, and decorating them with rocks from the gravel by the cistern. The mailman drives up and brings two big boxes to the door.

"Mike run to the garden and tell Mama," I yell. Mike hollers, "Mama, Mama, the mailman is here and he's got boxes." Mama comes up stripping off her gloves and wiping the dirt from her dress as she walks.

Mama thanks the mailman and he tips his hat and leaves. She washes her hands in the washbowl in the kitchen while we impatiently watch.

"Can I open one?" I ask. I'm eyeing the largest one sitting on the floor by the kitchen table covered in a yellow oil cloth.

"Yes." She hands me a paring knife. "Be careful."

I'm so excited to see what wonderful things are in the boxes. I know they're school clothes for all of us— shirts, blouses, dresses, pants, and shoes.

I wonder if my friend Joyce from Sunday school is getting new school clothes.

Joyce is a plump little blond girl with blue eyes who is soft and gentle. She is as quiet and polite as I am noisy and lively. She doesn't do stuff or always get in trouble like me. When we go to town on Saturday nights to sell eggs and cream, I search for Joyce. We walk up and down the streets, and in and out of the cafes where the grownups sit drinking coffee, eating big pieces of pie, or drinking beer.

There are two cafes—one is narrow like a train car filled with high-top booths and shiny pink and black tile. It is busy and loud with the laughter of the farm women catching up on the gossip. They collect the money from the eggs and cream, buy groceries for the next week, then catch up on what's new. The other cafe has a long, long counter, a few booths and a big dance floor with pool tables in one corner.

§

Kenny and Daphne leave at the end of summer. I wave until a cloud of dust swallows them up. Their room feels emptier than when they came. "Why did they have to leave?" I asked Daddy.

"Kenny wants to go to California—everything good is in California."

Then why aren't we in California?

"Why don't you go to the grove and help Ted and Mike carry some wood to the woodpile; we're going to need a lot of it soon." We burn wood in the cookstove in the kitchen and the potbellied stove in the living room.

I can cut wood now. The axe is sharp so Daddy tells me, "Be careful not to cut off your foot." I feel good when I'm chopping wood. I feel like I'm winning in a contest nobody knows about but me.

Chapter Eight

Ladies Aid

Sometimes I watch Mama stand by the tall window in the living room looking out at the long winding dirt road, watching for Daddy's headlights.

Where is Daddy?

"Mama, are you alright?"

She nods and says, "Let's go make some cookies." But it seems like she's got things on her mind, even when she tucks us into bed, even when she hears our prayers.

Bill often asks, "Tell us a story, Mama."

"Okay, okay, but just one. I'm busy."

Mama's magic bedtime stories tell us about when she was little. They are filled with sleigh rides, fairytale Christmases, and Valentines boxes filled with yummy chocolates and good surprises. She tells us about the wonderful grandparents who came and lived with them and aunts and uncles too. Her eyes are dreamy when she talks about her mother, the grandmother I never met. "She was so kind, so wonderful, so gentle, but she was sick most of the time. She had ten children. When two died it broke her heart."

Mama goes to Ladies Aid at our church every Wednesday afternoon. One hot July Wednesday I beg to go with her. I just want to be with Mama alone without any other kids hanging on her.

"No, I need you to stay here and help Daddy take care of the little kids."

I find Daddy out in the barnyard working on our old-new tractor that always is breaking down. I wind my arms around his waist and look up into his beautiful blue-green eyes. "Daddy, Mama's going to Ladies Aid. Make her take me with her. She says I can't go because I have to help you."

"I'll see what I can do. Get back to the house and help her now." Handing me a tool, he says, "Here, put this wrench in the truck on your way to the house." I open the truck door and a bottle of whisky rolls out from under the seat. I carefully put it back under the seat alongside a couple sticks of dynamite, and lay the wrench right under the steering wheel where Daddy will see it.

Daddy comes in the house and washes his hands in the blue enamel pan in the sink, while mama hustles around putting homemade bread, fried potatoes, thick slices of ham, and canned tomatoes from last year on the table. Taking a sip of his coffee he says to her, "I think when you go to town this afternoon you should take Bubbles with you."

"She needs to help you with the kids," Mama says.

"I can manage for a few hours," Daddy answers back.

"Get your clothes changed then because I'm leaving," she barks at me. I hurry, excited because I never get Mama to myself. Mama doesn't talk to me all the way to town. When we get to the church she says, "Be a lady and remember children are to be seen and not heard."

Ladies Aid is so boring that I feel sorry I came. I hear the women read the Bible, watch silently while they get out the cookies and tea, and listen while they gossip about everybody in the county who isn't there. They say some mean things about Joyce's mama because she doesn't go to church, and they talk on about others.

"I wonder where Berniece is today?"

"I wonder if Ruth's husband came back?"

I hear them talk about their new cars in voices that sound like they think they are better than us.

And I hear Mama say, "That's wonderful. I'm so happy for you."

"How's Lon doing? I hear he's been sick?" a lady asks.

"No, he's just fine, thank you," Mama answers back.

I hate the pukey way they treat her. My heart feels like it could burst with all the love I feel for her. Right then I despise Ladies Aid. *When I grow up I will never, ever go there.*

§

Tomorrow is the start of my fourth year in school. I hardly slept all night because my friend, Jacki, who had her last year, says Mrs. Foster is really mean. She's a tall, no-nonsense, old woman who doesn't let kids fool around. I'm scared of her. *What if she gets mad at me? Will she spank me?*

I give her no reason to spank me, but Ted gets a board on his butt.

Mrs. Foster reads from the Bible or from a Bible
storybook, every day after lunch. I don't really listen
when she reads. I have important things to think about. I
wonder why Mama was mad last night after Daddy got
home. I think about Bernie and if he's okay at home
without me to comfort him. I wonder what we are going
to have for supper tonight. Every day we go home for
lunch but I'm always hungry by recess.

§

I'm counting the days until Thanksgiving when we
can stay home four days. Mama's been baking and
storing up cookies, pies and cakes for weeks. Finally it
comes and we celebrate with Aunt Helen. This day is
unusually warm and sunny and we are able to play
outside in our shirt sleeves. Before Charlene and I can go
out we have to wash all the dishes. Mama fills the dish
pan with hot water, then brings the yucky plates a few at
a time. I wash while Charlene dries with a spotless white
dish towel Mama hands her from the towel drawer. Aunt
Helen sits at the table breastfeeding her most recent
baby. The pile of dirty dishes seems endless to eight year
old me and six year old Charlene. When it comes to the
pots and pans I am relieved and grateful to hear Mama
say, "Okay girls you can go play now, I will finish up."

§

Two days before Christmas we wake to a gently
falling snow. The pristine whiteness covers up the brown

countryside and makes everything beautiful. We walk the short distance to school. Ted makes snowballs and lobs them at me while I try to catch snowflakes on my tongue. By end of the school day the wind has picked up and we hustle home to get away from the assault of biting snow on our faces. By Christmas Eve day, the snow has picked up force. When I look out the window I see deep drifts forming in the yard.

Mama is worried. "How are we going to get to church?" she asks my daddy. "I have a solo and the kids have parts in the Christmas pageant." I can tell she's afraid we won't be able to get to town. Daddy answers her, "I will get the team and wagon ready, you find quilts and lots of warm clothes and we'll just do it the old fashioned way."

Sure enough after a hot soup supper, we put on all our warm clothes, while Daddy brings the team and wagon up to the back door. We pile in with quilts and pillows—our noses barely stick out of the covers. We ride the four miles to church in a rickety old wooden wagon listening to Daddy cluck and call out to the horses, "Come on Diamond, that's a boy, easy now easy."

Mama's friend, Mrs. Kern lives across the street from the church. Daddy parks the horses in her front yard. Inside the-church we celebrate the birth of Christ by acting out the Christmas story and Mama sings *Star of the East* and *Silent Night* in her beautiful soprano voice. At midnight we step out of the church into a raging blizzard. We can barely see the cars lined up in front when Daddy goes to get the horses. Mrs. Kern, invites us to spend the night. Mama and Daddy bring in all the quilts from the wagon and make us kids a bed on the living room floor. The boys and I snuggle in together, still wearing our clothes, while Mama and Daddy use a roll away bed set up in the parlor. We are all worried that Santa Claus won't find us, but Mama says he won't let us down and when we get home he will have been there.

I'm not happy with this situation but I'm helpless to do anything about it. In spite of my fretting, I fall asleep on the hard floor. When we wake up in the morning the blizzard has stopped. We gather up our belongings and pile in the wagon to head for home. It's a cold, crystal clear morning, piles of snow are everywhere.-Smoke billows out of the chimneys of all the houses in town, and the few houses we pass on the way home. We munch on the cookies and fruitcake Mrs. Kern gave us when Daddy refused her offer of breakfast. As the horses trudge through the deep snow toward home we seem to be the only people in the world on this Christmas morning.

Finally the horses plod up our drive way and Daddy lets us pile out of the wagon in front of the back door. "Go upstairs." he says "And don't you dare look at your stockings until I get in the house. I want to see what Santa brought too."

We obediently climb the stairs. It's cold up here, so we snuggle in the biggest bed altogether laughing and fighting over covers. It seems like forever before we hear him say, "OK kids you can come down now.

When I walk in the living room I am star struck seeing beneath my stocking a small white satin lined basket holding the beautiful baby doll that I asked Santa for weeks ago. She has real curly hair, eyes that open and shut, and is wearing a white lace dress and tiny little shoes. I love her the minute I see her.

§

The snow piles up on our dirt road. On the days Mrs. Foster can't get her old black car through the snowdrifts to get back and forth to school, she stays at our house and sleeps with me, because it is me or the broken-down couch. I stay as far away from her big old body as possible. Sometimes I get over so far, I fall off the bed. I hate sleeping with my teacher. Yuck. One time she rubbed my bare bottom and then pulled my nightgown down to cover it. My teacher!

Time slowly travels through one cold month after another until May appears with sunshine, budding trees and blooming flowers. The last day of school is a blissfully warm day. Walking home I can hear the meadowlarks and the killdeers chirping and singing. I am day dreaming of hot days, going barefoot—climbing trees—capturing birds—riding my horse, and going to bed when I feel like it.

Chapter Nine

The Apple

The fresh air is soft like satin on my face. On my early morning trip to the outhouse the ground feels warm on my bare feet. Life is wonderful at the moment. All is well.

Daddy stayed out in the field on the tractor all night. I run to hug him as he pulls the tractor into the barnyard. His face and clothes are streaked with dirt and he gets off the tractor like a crippled old man.

"There's my girl," he says as I run to hug him. "Stop it, sweetheart, you're going to get all dirty." Too late, I'm already wrapped around him. My pedal-pushers and shirt now look like I rolled in the yard.

I eat Mama's wonderful pancakes and run for the barn to see the new kittens and old Bird. Ted is already there, getting out the saddle. I grab a kitten and take it to the house to show Mama. She pets the kitten then says, "Clean your room and change the sheets. It's Saturday."

Mama washes my hair on Saturdays using dish soap. She curls it with rag strips torn from an old pillowcase. I try to sit quietly while she takes a lock of hair, rolls it around the strip and ties the rag in a knot. I run around all day, looking like something out of a freak show with rags flapping in my face.

Daddy loves my "chestnut hair." He always says, "You sure look pretty in those curls. Bet all the boys will be after you tonight."

But when I look in the mirror, I see an ugly, skinny little face with sunken eyes, a big nose, and lots of freckles. I hate the freckles because every adult in my life teases me all the time about the "fly specs" all over my face and arms.

"You have to suffer to be beautiful," Mama says, when I complain about her rolling my hair too tight, or when I complain about having to wear shoes when we leave the farm for church. My shoes are too small for my spread-out bare feet.

Mama tells me how she uses buttermilk on her face every night to keep her skin white. Together we brush our hair one hundred strokes to make it thick before I go upstairs to bed. She tells me to never wash my face with water, because water causes wrinkles. She shows me how to use lard on my face as a cleansing cream and carefully wipe it off with a soft cloth.

I don't even know there is such a thing as a toothbrush or toothpaste until my cousin Bobbie asks, "Don't you guys brush your teeth?"

§

When family comes, the rafters in our little house threaten to explode with noise and laughter. People and more people are everywhere, laughing and talking over each other. There are Daddy's three plump sisters:

proper Aunt Pearl; fun Aunt Ella; bubbly Aunt Blanche, and their skinny husbands, along with ten or twelve cousins. They come in what Mama calls "redneck carloads," with suitcases tied on top, loaded with food, and feather-tick pillows and blankets. They're like a horde of hungry elephants, swarming like ants, filling the house. They chuckle, chortle, and tell stories. Mama calls it "cornbread-and-hominy-grit humor."

Mama and the aunts cook black-eyed peas, dandelion greens, side pork, and tons of fried potatoes, gravy, and corn on the cob. We eat mountains of fried chicken, and homemade bread with jams and jellies that Aunt Ella brought. Daddy makes the biscuits and gravy.

Daddy and I look forward to their coming every year. Mama's okay with it but dreads the extra work. The laughter and love they bring is welcome but it brings a different kind of craziness.

Once when Daddy's whole family came, they brought an Ouija board. Everybody, including the children, got to ask it questions. It gave me a spooky feeling. And what they did next gave me cold chills. Two card tables with four adults at each played a game called Tables Up. Each adult rubbed their hands together for friction and then placed both hands on the table in front of them repeating over and over "Tables up, tables up" until the tables rose off the floor and hung wobbling in the air. There was a contest to see who could get the tables up first. I didn't watch long, the yard with the other kids was calling me.

Outside, we hear the adults talking and laughing through the open windows and swinging doors as they play cards and drink cold tea or coffee. Nights are warm, balmy, with bright moonlight and twinkling stars. Nobody has to go to bed. We play into the dark under the stars.

One by one, the little kids get sleepy and go inside. Not me, not Ted, not Bobbie, or Loretta or Shirley, or Maxine, or Gail. We sit in the car and tell ghost stories. I shiver happily as the older kids take turns coming up with tales of figures that spin through the air or witches in the cellar. Loretta, way older than the rest of us, is the best yarn teller. She makes up stories that make us all shiver and we lock the car doors.

In the middle of the night, aunts, uncles, and cousins are sleeping all over the house. My bed goes to Aunt Ella and Uncle George. The boys' room is for Aunt Pearl and Uncle Rob. Aunt Blanche and Uncle Henry sleep on a feather-tick on the floor in the living room with little cousins flopped around them. Arms, legs, and little bodies are everywhere on the floor, on the couch and in chairs. This time they stay a week. Daddy only goes to town once to buy groceries.

As exciting as it is to see them come, we all breathe a tired sigh of relief when everybody rounds up their kids, piles their masses of dirty clothes and luggage into their cars and drive off. The house feels strangely empty and not quite real.

§

But there's no time to think about it. There is bedding to wash in the wringer washer and to hang on the wire clotheslines, beds to make, pots, pans and dishes to return to their rightful places, floors to be scrubbed and waxed.

It is the last hurrah of summer. School starts next week and it's time to get ready. There are no new clothes coming in the mail this year, no new shoes or coats. "We have to make do," Mama says as she sews all day on the machine. Daddy patches the soles of our shoes on a rusty piece of iron with a foot-shape on top, and polishes them the best he can. Aunt Dorothy brings me an old brown coat. I love it because it smells like her.

§

It's October and still really warm so we kids are outside. We're not supposed to slide down the straw stacks. Daddy and Mama said never slide down the straw stacks because it's dangerous. But the tall mountain of fresh, sweet straw was a temptation we couldn't resist. "I'll do it if you will," Ted said.

"You little kids don't tell!" I help Bill and Mike climb the mountain of straw. We all slid down once and then we heard Mama calling. It was hard to hide what we've been doing when we came in the kitchen with our hair and jeans full of straw.

Daddy took a load of grain to the elevator in town to sell this afternoon. His truck pulls back in the driveway, just as the sun is going down. When he comes hustling in the door with arms full of groceries, I can see he's pleased with himself.

"Kids, come look!" In the wooden grain wagon behind his truck are two bicycles, a big one for me and Ted and a small one for the little guys.

"Yay!" we yell. Ted is already up in the wagon when Mama says, "They can't have these until tomorrow. They're not good kids. They've been sliding down the new straw stacks. They've been told repeatedly how deathly dangerous, this is." Mama turns to us and says, "You could get buried alive and suffocate."

"So you've been in the straw. How many times do we have to tell you, kids suffocate and die in straw stacks?" Daddy whips off his belt. "Line up here boys." Ted, Mike, Bill and Bernie obey and take their places against the white kitchen wall.

In panic I look at Mama. *Isn't she going to do anything to stop him?* Quick like a cat's tongue, Daddy gets one flick of the belt at Ted before I jump in between them and take the belt away from him.

Daddy sort of shakes his head like he is trying to figure out what just happened and walks away. In a weird, sick way I feel I am stronger than Mama. For the first time I realize how much power I have. Later when I am in bed I think, *Nobody is in charge of this circus. It's all up to me.*

The next morning, we get to have the bicycles. The big one is a boy's bike, of course, and I fall off, and fall off, and fall off. I land on the bar several times, making my "whoo-whoo" black and blue. Ted jumps on the bike and masters it in no time.

"I never saw anybody as determined to ride a bike as you are. I sure didn't think you could do it" Mama says to me. I never wondered why she didn't help me.

§

One March afternoon when we get home from school, Mama's brothers Bud and Orville, big, strong, bald-headed guys who love to tease all their nieces and nephews, are sitting on the couch in our living room.

"Go outside and play," Mama says. "And take the boys with you."

After our uncles leave, we come in as Mama is starting supper. Mama is quiet and has a funny look on her face. "Set the table and wash the boy's hands," she orders.

When Daddy comes in for supper, he looks at Mama and asks, "What did your brothers want?"

"I'll tell you later." Mama doesn't look at him.

The next morning Daddy yells at me. "What is wrong with you? Do you know how much trouble you caused?"

What did I do? My stomach feels sick when I see how angry he is.

"Am I such a poor dad that you have to steal food? I don't care if you're starving, don't ever steal—ever! Do you hear me?"

I stole an apple from Nadine's lunch box last week. I didn't think about it, I just took it. I didn't mean to do it. We were outside for recess when Nadine had a bloody

nose and asked me to go inside and get her a
handkerchief out of her lunchbox. When I opened the
lunch box, the apple was just sitting there and I took it.
Nadine told our teacher who looked for it and it wasn't
there.

"Why did you take it?" the teacher asked me.

"Because I was hungry."

I never thought it would go any further than that. But
the teacher must have told somebody. Now Daddy is
mad at me.

"That was wrong," Daddy shouts. "What would
make you do something like that?"

"It just happened. I didn't think she wanted it."

"Your uncles were here yesterday asking your
mother if we have enough food to eat."
He looked away but his eyes still looked angry when he
said, "And your mother's family already hates me."

"I'm sorry, Daddy." I threw my arms around his neck
looking for comfort. *I am so terrible. Please hold me.*

"Why do they hate you?"

"Because I married your mother. Now get dressed for
school and don't you ever do anything like that again."

Chapter Ten

Bad News

It's still October with perfect fall weather—warm sun and a soft breeze. We all know winter could hit at any moment.

Rather than race each other home, we walk slowly, carrying books, and dragging our jackets. I hear whip-poor-wills and meadowlarks, and step around the badger holes in the dusty dirt road.

As we break into a run at the driveway, Ted yells, "Race you!" The smell of fresh baked bread and cinnamon rolls, hits our noses before we even open the back door. Throwing our books and coats down we lunge for the bounty. Homemade buns with peanut butter and jelly or round, thick cinnamon rolls will hold us until supper.

I look out the kitchen window to see a long, sleek brown car slowly coming up the drive.

"You kids pick up your stuff quick, the minister is here." Mama is waving her arms as she speaks. Falling all over each other, we grab our books and sweaters and hide them on the stairwell. We don't want Mama to be embarrassed.

I peek out the windows as Reverend Butts get out of the car, stands for a moment, straightens up his shoulders and walks quickly to the door.

"Come in, Reverend," Mama says to our pastor who has his hat in his hands.

He says something to Mama and she sags against the door frame. He helps her to a kitchen chair. Mama says, "Ted go to the hayfield and get Dad."

When Ted looks like he wants to finish his peanut butter and jelly sandwich first, she says in a voice that sounds strange, "Now!" Mama is crying. I've never seen her cry before.

"Shush," I say to the little guys, as we sit at the table waiting. I'm suddenly aware of the peanut butter from the hot roll dripping down my chin, and I swipe at it with my hand, my stomach queasy. *Something is wrong.*

Reverend Butts sits quietly by Mama, staring at something out the window.

Daddy hustles in the door all dusty and dirty with a worried look on his face.

"Dad is dead," Mama squeaks at him through her tears. He gathers her in his arms. The minister now stands awkwardly.

"We'll make plans tomorrow," he says.

Granddaddy Jim is dead. Now I really feel sick as I hustle the little kids outside so Daddy can be alone with Mama. "Our granddaddy died," I tell them. I am so sad.

We sit at the side of the house, petting the dog, and watch the minister drive away. The next day we go to school as usual and no one says anything more to us about him.

Mama and Daddy go to the funeral. "No kids allowed," Mama says. After that It's like Granddaddy Jim never even lived.

Sitting at the supper table one night I ask, "What happened to Granddaddy Jim?"

Mama yells at me. "You know what happened. Don't ask stupid questions."

"Don't yell at her," Daddy says.

"Well, she's just trying to hurt me."

My heart does a scolded dog jump and my stomach sinks to the floor. *Why would I try to hurt Mama?* Confused, I feel a heavy pain settle in my chest.

Chapter Eleven

A Dangerous Man

Wally turns up about spring planting time. Daddy found him downtown, looking for a job. Wally is a slim, handsome man, with broad shoulders, a foot taller than Daddy. But Mama always says, "Everybody is a foot taller than my five-foot-seven-inch husband."

Wally looks like Clark Gable, with his dark wavy hair, dark wire-brush mustache, a sort of Slick Willie grin, and dark eyes.

Mama doesn't like him much and is suspicious of him from the start. "I feel creepy around him," I hear her tell Daddy. But it's time for spring calving, pigging and planting, so Daddy keeps him on.

Wally gets my bedroom and I sleep on a cot in the boy's room. He doesn't spend much time in the house, as he works in the fields dawn to dusk or goes to town with Daddy. When supper comes, he eats quietly. Sometimes he says, "Mrs. Jones, not only are you beautiful, you are the best cook in the country."

Mama looks at him like he is crazy. She isn't hungry for compliments like I am because Daddy tells her every day that she is "beautiful, wonderful, and the best ever woman in the world." That's why it's confusing when he says horrible things to her some nights.

Wally and Daddy talk farm talk when supper is over. They lean back in their chairs, Wally lights a cigarette, Daddy lights his pipe, and they drink coffee while Mama and I clear the table. Sometimes when I walk by him, he smiles and hands me a stick of gum or a piece of candy. "Our secret," he whispers.

This summer is like all the other summers, the torture of vacation Bible school, hot days on the horse, church on Sundays, town on Saturday nights, company pouring in, and then more company as relatives descend on us— their cars kicking up puffs of dust from our rutted dirt road.

§

I'm in fifth grade this year. The days fly by as school is fun with our new teacher, Miss Ruby, who doesn't care if we learn anything or not. I read books all day, the other kids quietly do their own thing. She doesn't pay much attention to us. Each family takes a turn bringing hot lunch for everybody. Our day is always Friday.

Before I know it, Christmas is here. We can't have a tree until a week before Christmas, "Because of the fire danger," Mama says. She can't put lights on the tree like Aunt Dorothy does, because we don't have a generator to make electricity like they do.

Aunt Dorothy's tree is so beautiful with all the flashy midnight-blue balls, sparkling icicles, and blinking lights. Under the tree are packages that look like they'll be amazing, glorious surprises for our cousins, Butch and Terry.

Our tree is scraggly, decorated with colored construction paper chains that we made, sugar cookies hanging by strings, and cranberry chains that took us a long time to string on a thread. We do have a few colored balls with glitter on them. The whole mess is covered with silver icicles that we kids lobbed on it. A few small packages lie under the tree.

§

Valentine's Day arrives with homemade hearts, lacy paper doilies, and carefully chosen penny Valentines for the kids in school. The Monday afterwards we are yelling and screaming at each other with the joy of freedom as we race home starving and looking for our usual snack. The sun is already fading and the wind cuts through our coats like a sharp knife with a frozen blade.

"Bubbles, wait for me," Bill says.

"Hurry up! Ted is home already. Here, let me carry your books."

I feel cozy standing by the warm cookstove as we stuff our mouths with warm oatmeal cookies. We're all talking to Mama at once when suddenly she drops her cookie and screams. She's scrambling for the living room, when a waft of smoke meets my nose.

Fire! The clothes hanging on a wooden rack next to the potbellied stove in the living room are on fire. Mama grabs the rack and screams, "Open the door." She drags the burning clothes rack covered with a pile of burning clothes out the door and throws them on the snowbank, then comes back in for another load. The house fills up with ugly black smoke. We cough and choke while we stand wide-eyed watching her. I'm holding Bernie and Mike is holding the door open. Ted is trying to help Mama.

"Ted, get your horse. Go get Dorothy," Mama says when the fire is all in the snowbank. The house is filled with smoke and is freezing cold from the wide-open door.

Ted races to the barnyard, grabs a horse, and doesn't even put a saddle on it. He tears out to the dirt road, kicking and hitting the horse furiously. Aunt Dorothy lives two miles away. The wait seems endless while Mama sits moaning in the kitchen as we huddle together, shivering in silence.

Aunt Dorothy comes flying up the driveway in her junky pick-up, a faded green bucket of bolts. Ted is with her. She puts stuff on Mama's arms and stomach. She helps clean up the mess. Mama's face is twisted with pain. Aunt Dorothy watches over Mama but doesn't know what else to do. She picks up the phone and yells at my cousin Terry to go find my uncle Bud so he can go find my daddy.

More waiting. My head is aching, gnawing, throbbing in panic. *What can I do? What can I do?* I keep the little guys quiet and away from Mama. My gut churns. I feel like I'm right in the center of her terrible pain. I want desperately to help but I can't do anything but stare at the ugly red marks spreading across her arms and face.

Daddy walks in the door, his face looking afraid. He gently wraps Mama in a blanket, picks her up in his arms and lays her in the car. I follow him to the car waving for him to take her purse.

"Take care of the boys, I'll be back as soon as I can. You kids pray."

Pray? To a God I can't see? Huh. A God who killed his own Son? I saw the movies at church of Jesus hanging on the cross. I heard what the minister said about all of us being sinners and worthless pieces of flesh. *What's the use of praying?*

I stand and kick at a rock and the pain in my foot helps clear the pain in my head as the car leaves the driveway. I decide in a moment, quick as lightning, that a woman's life is just too hard and thankless. *I don't want to be a woman. I will never, ever, be like my mother. I mean never. I will not sew, I will not can food, I will not garden, I will not stay home while my husband is off somewhere.*

I am so scared, but then a huge anger takes over and fills me and I swear under my breath at a God I can't see. Before we moved in, I felt that there was *an unseen evil hiding in this house, and now I know it's true.*

Beautiful, dark-haired, boyish Aunt Dorothy, my favorite person in the whole world other than Daddy, comes over. She says, "Get some clothes together you're all coming home with me."

I usually like going to Aunt Dorothy's house. It's pretty there with big overstuffed chairs and a pale leather couch. It's warm and cozy and not poor and messy like our house.

Uncle Bud is usually a big tease, but this night he looks at us like he feels really sorry for us. Aunt Dorothy makes a bed for us on the floor and we sleep huddled together, except for Ted who is up on the couch.

The next day Aunt Dorothy takes us to school. Daddy is home when school gets out, trying to clean up the burned linoleum. As he scrubs the smoky wall he tells us, "Mama is going to be in the hospital for a long time." No one tells us the real truth.

"Bubbles you have to help me with the boys now and take care of Bernie. We have to keep the house clean and the dishes washed. I'll do the cooking," Daddy says.

"Okay, Daddy, but the boys have to help."

"You tell them what to do, I'll make them do it."

Lucky for us Daddy is a good cook. He hires some neighbor girls (Marcela, eighteen and in the eighth grade, and Mary-Lou, sixteen and in the seventh grade) to come home with us after school. They help clean the house and stay with us when Daddy goes to visit Mama. Wally does the field work, takes care of the livestock and helps Ted milk the cows.

"Stop yelling at Ted," Daddy says when he hears me yell up the stairs.

Ted is acting like brat. "Daddy, he won't help me find Mike's shoes. We're going to be late for school again."

The kitchen is a warm cocoon of sausage smells and perking coffee. Daddy has set out hot cereal and milk on the table. Heavy white bowls that don't match are waiting for hungry, gobbling mouths. Bernie is sitting in his high chair banging the tray with a spoon. Daddy flips the sausage on the plate without missing.

When I go to put the sausage on the table, Daddy looks right at me and says, "If you fight with your brothers, God will come and take one of them away."

Oh no! I not only have to watch over my brothers, I have to protect them from God too. This is too hard.

I want to see Mama so bad that the feeling settles in my chest and I can't think straight. I sit in school feeling like an orphan, like I've been left alone, and like no one wants me.

At home I try to keep the little boys from being too lonely. I remind them to wash their hands and faces, and change their clothes. At night, I listen to their prayers.

When I go to bed, I pull the sheet up around my shoulders, stick my thumb in my mouth and suck it until I fall to sleep. Daddy says, "You have to be brave and help me." He tells everyone what a great help I am to him. But each day seems longer than the one before. I am eaten up with worry.

Did Mama die and no one told us?

The hospital won't let us in to see her. "Too much danger of infection," Daddy tells us.

One Saturday Daddy tells us to get in the old gray Dodge. We can ride along to the hospital with him and Mama will look out the window and wave at us.

The thirty miles to the hospital is a long squabbling ride. "Are we there yet?" one of the little boys asks every few minutes. Daddy and Wally ride in the front seat talking about crops and cattle. We five are squished on the dusty gray back seat. Ted gets one window and I get the other and the little ones are squished in between.

"Ow, you're crushing me."

"Get over, I can't stand your stinky breath."

"I can't see out the window."

"Pig."

"Stupid."

"Fat slob.

"You're stomping on my foot."

"Get off me you sow."

"Stop pinching me, wart face."

I put Bernie on my lap to protect him and give the others more space. He climbs around on me, hugging my neck and messing up my dress. I don't care; he's my baby.

"Stop it you guys. Right now! Don't make me stop this car. Why don't you sing some songs or something?" Daddy sounds mad.

I give Ted my best snarky glare because he's pinching Mike and we start in on a favorite. "You are my sunshine, my only sunshine, you make me happy when skies are gray." We don't sing very well, but make up for it by singing loud. Then it's, "Jesus loves me this I know for the Bible tells me so. Little ones to him belong, we are weak but he is strong . . ." The little guys start singing, "The B-I-B-L-E, yes that's the book for me, I stand alone on the word of God, the B-I-B-L-E."

When Ted starts "Ninety-nine bottles of beer on the wall, ninety-nine bottles of beer, if one those bottles should happen to fall, ninety-eight bottles of beer on the wall," Daddy says, "Okay, okay, that's enough."

Finally, Daddy parks the car in front of the hospital. "Watch that window right there," he says, pointing up to second floor, before he disappears into the big brick building. We watch with our necks bent back and our heads craned toward the sky.

By the time Mama comes and sticks her head out the window, my neck is aching from the strain. She waves a handkerchief and blows kisses and relief washes over me. I feel a mixture of joy and an intense longing to be near her and hear her voice.

It's a warm day and we wrestle on the lawn. We do some foot races down the sidewalk, practice cartwheels, and play statue in the grass. In statue, you grab somebody by the wrists and swing them around and around until you get up a lot a speed and then let go. They have to freeze just the way they land and see how long they can stay that way.

I lean against a post to catch my breath. Wally rolls down the car window.

"Bubbles, why don't you come sit in the car and have a candy bar with me? It's nice in here." Tired of the roughhousing, I get in the car.

Wally unwraps a Hersey and hands me half.

"How old are you?"

"Nine."

"Then you're old enough. I have something to tell you but you can never tell anyone I told you this."

"Okay."

Putting his hand on my knee he says, "Do you know anything about sex?"

"No," I say slowly. I feel dumb because he's staring at me. I drop my eyes and look at my shoes. A shiver runs through me. *My shoes are muddy. Why didn't I polish them before we left?*

It feels as if my ears are being pulled toward Wally, by his soft voice and my curiosity.

"Men have peters and women have pussies."

What? Kittens?

"And when men and women get together, they take off all their clothes and the man sticks his peter in the pussy between the woman's legs."

Why would a woman have a cat between her legs?

"This is called screwing."

Get out, get out, don't listen to this. Move.

"You're a foxy, pretty girl, so soft and lovely . . . all the guys are going to want to screw you."

I shouldn't listen to this, I should open the door and run. But he's a grown-up. I feel stuck to the seat by the power of words I never hear: *foxy, pretty, lovely.* My breath is sucked into my chest and comes out in short gasps.

"I like to screw Marcela when I'm at her house working for her dad. Marcela really likes it. Someday you will have breasts. Boys really like to touch girl's breasts."

Don't listen to this. Your shoes are really ugly. You forgot to polish them. Did Mama see how bad they look?

I can't say anything to Wally. He's an adult and children do not talk back to adults or even question them.

The boys who are still tumbling around on the grass seem miles away. Then, as if in a dream, I see Daddy rounding them up.

Wally says, "Tonight, when we drop you guys off at the movie theater, you go inside and wait for a little bit. Let your brothers get seated, then go outside around to the back and I'll be waiting for you by the outhouse. I'll have a wonderful surprise for you. I'll show you what I've been talking about."

Intrigued by the idea of a surprise and full of curiosity I agree. "Okay."

Seeing Daddy coming, I feel relieved knowing I'll be free from the trap of Wally. I feel guilty for listening to him, but still I'm curious. I tumble breathless out of the passenger side so Wally can scoot over.

Daddy, who's wearing his best suit, a white shirt and tie for Mama, looks happy as he gets in the driver's seat. The boys pile in the middle of the back seat smelling like sweat and dirt. I sit pressing my face to the window thinking about what I've just heard.

Daddy stops at a gas station and fills up the tank. He walks in to pay for the gas and comes out with treats—pop, chips, and pinwheels on a stick. I hold my pinwheel up and blow on it to make the reds, purples, pinks and blues all flow together and we start down the road.

"Dad, make her roll up her window. We're cold."

Just as Ted says this, a gust of wind grabs my pinwheel. I watch helplessly as it skips from the ditch, hops over the fence into the field and disappears in the wind. Sobbing, I roll up my window.

Wally turns around. "You big crybaby, crying over a little thing like that. You should be ashamed of yourself."

Is Daddy really going to let Wally talk to me like this? My heart turns to stone. Acid rage springs up in my gut. *I'll show him. He's not my friend anymore. I won't have anything more to do with him.* I sit silently in the backseat plotting how I'm going to get back at him.

When we reach the theater, Daddy gives Ted money to pay the twelve cents for each of our tickets. He says, "There's enough money for popcorn. Be sure everybody gets some."

The movie theater is a dark, mysterious place with rows and rows of velvet seats. I walk in and sit down with Mike and Bill, feeling smug. *I don't care about any old surprise. I wonder how long Wally will wait out in the dark for me to show up. Serves him right for being so mean.*

When Daddy picks us up from the movie, Wally sits talking to him and doesn't look at me.

§

On Monday when Marcela and Mary Lou come home with us after school, I tell them what Wally said.

Marcela's big body looms over me in her faded cotton housedress. She grabs me by the shoulders and says, "You gotta tell your daddy."

Stop, stop, leave me alone you're hurting me.

"You gotta tell your daddy."

"I can't," I whimper.

"You have to. You have to tell your daddy. Tonight. Promise you'll tell your daddy—tonight."

"No, I can't."

"Yes, you can. This is not right. He's a bad man. Stay away from him. You tell him now—tonight. If you don't, you'll be sorry." *She must not like him as much as Wally said she did.*

"Could you tell him?"

"No, you have to. And you have to do it tonight," Mary Lou chimes in. Both are talking at once and keep saying I must tell Daddy what Wally said.

I can't make sense of this. What happened anyway? Am I just making a big deal out of this? Will Daddy be mad at me? Why did I even tell Marcela and Mary Lou?

When Daddy drives in, they push me out the door. "Tell him." Shivering in the cold dark night, I stand in front of the garage. I try to tell Daddy, but I can't get any words out. I stammer, and hear my heart pounding hard in my chest.

"Uh, Daddy, Marcela told me . . . uh . . . I have ta tell you that . . . uh, Wally is . . . uh, a bad man . . . and he uh . . . said some stuff." That's all I can get out. *Please don't be mad at me,* I think.

Daddy seems to be thinking about something as we get in the car to take Marcela and Mary Lou home. When he tucks me into bed, he puts his hand on my head and says, "Don't worry, sweetheart. Mama will be coming home soon and we'll talk then."

After that night Marcela and Mary Lou are always at our house or I am at their house with them.

§

Old Bird is gone. One day Daddy loaded her up in a truck and drove away. Ted says she's going where old horses go to die. I have too much on my mind to take on any more sadness, so I shove the pain away.

A couple of days later, four new horses are in the yard. Belle is the one Daddy says is for me. She is a gentle, spotted-gray plodder, two barrels wide. My short legs barely fit across her back. I can't make her gallop like Bird did. Not wanting to hurt Daddy's feelings, I don't say what I am thinking. *I want a race horse not a plow horse.*

"Why can't I have the pinto?" I ask him.

"She's not broke to ride yet."

Ted got the dun-colored mare and the little kids got the Shetland pony. The plump spotted, brown-and-white Shetland has a temper. She tries to bite us and runs away every chance she gets. Her favorite trick is to go by a fence post and try to rub the rider off her back. She even lies down when she gets tired.

Daddy stops her from biting by using a special bit in the bridle. At least it isn't far to fall when she manages to dump one of us off so she can head for the barn.

Ted is busy breaking the pinto to lead, and patiently walks him around and around the barnyard. In the evening we watch the pinto try to buck Daddy off—horse legs pounding the dirt or shooting straight out in the air. It doesn't work. Daddy always wins.

"Here's how you *ear* a horse," he says. He throws his arms and legs up around the pinto's neck and bites her ear until she stands perfectly still.

The new horses help with the hole left by Mama being gone, but at night I am so lonely and I long for Mama. It seems like she's been away forever. Scary nightmares wake me and I'm up for hours fighting off voices. The voices say horrible things. Every cuss word I've ever heard sounds in my ears over and over. I hear whispers of *You're useless, no one can love you, give up, drop dead dummy, if you were gone no one would miss you.* Nights are torture to me.

Sleepily rubbing my eyes, I see Marcela standing at the stove where Daddy is usually cooking breakfast. *What is she doing here this time of day? Did she stay all night?*

Halfway through my pancakes, Daddy walks in the door. "You guys have a new baby brother," he says with a big smile.

What? No one even told us there was a baby coming. I can see Daddy's really excited. Ted is looking in the mirror over the sink, combing his wavy brown hair for school. "Not another baby" comes out of his mouth before he clamps his hand over it. I don't think Daddy heard him but I did.

Daddy tells me, "Put another big red x on the calendar." I find a crayon and mark April 23, 1947.

"We don't know what to name him. What do you guys think we should name him?" Daddy asks us.

I want to be helpful. Searching my brain for an answer, I come up with, "How about if we call him Jerry?" I'm reading a book in school about a boy named Jerry.

The next day, when Daddy walks in from the hospital he announces, "We named him Jerry Benson Jones."

My flat chest puffs out in pride. *He heard me. He liked the name!*

When Mama and Daddy walk in with the new baby, the first thing I want to see are the scars on her arms from the fire. Daddy told me, "Don't cry or make a fuss when you see them." But I couldn't even get close to her. I hold baby Jerry while all the little kids hug and hang on Mama.

She is home for one day when she lets it slip that she doesn't like the name Jerry. *It's my fault he'll be stuck with it for life.*

We finish our noon meal and it's time to scamper back to school. The boys fall all over each other going out the door. I'm in the porch when I hear, "Bubbles come back here." Mama's calling me.

"Come here." I walk to her chair and she pulls me down on her lap.

Oh, oh what did I do? Fear races through me. *This never happens.*

"What did Wally say to you?"

Filled with shame and afraid to tell her, I hide my face in her shoulder. *I can't tell her. Daddy's sitting right here.*

All I want to do is run. I squirm and try to get away, but I can't.

"Tell me. What did he say?"

I can't talk, I've never even heard the word sex in this house.

Daddy asks, "If I leave, will you tell her?"

I nod my head.

"Well?" she says, waiting for me to talk.

"He sorta told me about screwing and he said he does it to Marcela." The words come out in a burst of tears. *I know I've done something really bad.* I pull away and run up the stairs to find a place to hide.

Mama follows me up. "Is that all that happened?"

"Well, he wanted me to meet him while the boys went to the movie so he could show me what he was talking about—but I didn't."

Daddy plowed up the creaky stairs, "What is she saying?" he asks.

"She said that Wally is screwing Marcela and he wants to show her how it's done."

Mama's voice is steely, and the room is reeling around my head. *I have to get away.* Frantically I look at the doorway but Mama is standing in it.

Daddy starts pacing and yelling, and then yelling some more. Awful, horrible cuss words pour out of his mouth. He races downstairs for his shotgun and then races back upstairs. Red-faced and puffing, he waves the gun and yells, "I'm going to kill him!"

I'm terrified. *What have I done?* "Mama," I sob, "is he going to kill him?"

"No, he's not," she says calmly, "I have the car keys. He'll be all right. Just leave him alone for a while." Then she says gently, her voice, though tired, is kind and caring, "Someday you will learn that sex is a beautiful thing between a man and a woman who are married."

Baby Jerry is crying, and Mama whirls and leaves. Then she calls back up, "You haven't missed much school. You can still go."

Sucking it up, I wash my face, comb my hair, and run down the road to school. When I walk in, Miss Ruby asks, "Bubbles are you alright?"

"Just fine, thank you," I say politely.

It's as if I'm in a dream as I finish the afternoon and sit down for supper. No one says anything more. Daddy is calm, the boys have no clue anything is wrong. It's as if the ugly scene from earlier never happened. *Am I crazy? Did I imagine Daddy yelling and waving a shotgun?*

Two days later I can't believe my eyes when Wally is eating supper at our table, talking to Daddy about spring planting.

Huh? After all that screaming? It must not be that big a deal. I must not be that big a deal.

§

My mama's younger sister, Ruth, comes from Ohio to celebrate the fourth of July. Her husband Lewis drops her off and goes to Minnesota to see his sister. Aunt Ruth and my cousins Linda and Steve are staying a few days here and a few days at Aunt Helen's like they do every summer. Cousin Linda, about my age, sleeps with me.

Early one morning I hear the door to Wally's room creak noisily open. *That's weird.* Linda and I pull our bodies out of a messy, tousled bed and stumble out to the hall. Wally's door is open and he is lying on his bed buck naked with his peter straight up in the air.

Shocked, we run downstairs and tell Mama, who is holding baby Jerry in one arm and making pancakes with the other. "Lon," she says, "go up and see what Wally is doing." But, of course, by the time Daddy clomps up those squeaky stairs there is nothing to see.

"Ah there's nothin' there," he says when he clomps back down.

Linda and I shrug our shoulders and go off outside to see the kittens. She is scared of the cows, doesn't want to ride the horse, and doesn't know how to climb trees. In our back shed she tries to teach me some of the dance moves she's learned in her lessons in the city. We never really talk, but I learn a few moves, and I also get very jealous of her life.

I wonder how our mothers got to be sisters. Aunt Ruth is a glamour queen with long, pointy red nails, a black cigarette holder, whispery-soft silk blouses, ironed linen slacks, and rhinestone eyeglasses. She also has a loud screechy voice and pushes her opinions and yells her political beliefs at Mama. It doesn't seem to bother Mama all that much, but Aunt Helen always quakes when Aunt Ruth is around.

Linda's dad is a college professor, which puts Linda's mother in way higher society than the rest of us.

My Mama just loves her sister, but my Aunt Helen is one person around Mama and another around us. She turns her face into a sweet, I'll-do-anything-for-you servant when Aunt Ruth is around—and into a commanding officer when she's not.

"Good night nurse, Bubbles, what's wrong with you?" Aunt Helen says. "Why would you wear those old faded jeans? Go put on a dress and try to look presentable, and for God's sakes brush that bushy hair."

When Uncle Lewis comes after Aunt Ruth, all of Mama's family is waiting for him at our farm. We gather around his big old car filled with watermelon, cantaloupe, purple plums, and peaches. We haul it all to a bench set up in the shade, and gulp, devour, and gobble up all the sweetness with our hands—one final country-cousin hootenanny before we watch them drive down the road in Uncle Lewis' new sedan.

§

Daddy and Wally go to town right after breakfast. They don't come back for supper. They aren't here at bedtime. In the middle of the night I hear Mama walking the floor with the baby softly singing *Rock of Ages*. I know something is very wrong.

At breakfast Mama is groggy. Daddy isn't home. Mid-morning Daddy walks in with a black eye and a puffy, purple face. His rumpled blue shirt is spotted with something dark. *Is that blood?*

His words come out in a rush. "Edith sit down. I'll get my own coffee. It's been a long night. Wally clobbered me with a tire iron; knocked me out too. The sheriff finally found him hiding in the outhouse behind the theater. Wally is in jail."

Stunned by what Daddy is saying, all us kids stop what we are doing and stare.

"Go outside and play," Mama orders.

Through the open window, where I get most of my information, I hear Daddy saying to Mama, "No, she's not going to testify; it will ruin her."

A few days later the sheriff brings Wally out to get his clothes. From the living room window, I can see them out in the pasture across the dirt road, Daddy takes a cardboard box of clothes out to him. I want to go out and spit in his eye, for hurting my daddy, but Mama says we all have to stay in the house until he is gone. "He's dangerous," she says.

My insides suddenly flip, I am so afraid I can't move. *What if Wally blames me? What if he comes back and kills me?*

§

Now that Mama is home again, I can't wait to show her how well I can ride my new horse named Belle. I want to be a trick rider and learn how to jump on and off the way I've watched Dale Evans do in the movies. When I tell Mama my plans, she isn't the least bit encouraging, especially when I beg her to find someone to give me lessons.

"You, a trick rider? You can't walk across the room without falling over a chair."

She's right, I can't. I trip over my own big feet. Still, I continue to do my best to stand barefoot on Belle's slippery back, struggling to maintain my balance, riding a little way, and falling time after time, defeated and frustrated.

§

Farmers have a way of dropping in on each other on Sunday afternoons. Now that we have a new baby, neighbors come by and sit in our living room—a lot. Mama shows off the baby and I help serve them coffee and cake.

Hank and Josie tell a story of a woman from a town several miles away who disappeared during the winter. When the snow thawed, they found arms and legs and her head in a ditch. They cluck their tongues and shake their heads. Who could have done this horrible gruesome thing to her. Is he still at large?

From that conversation they wonder out loud who kidnapped the Lindberg Baby so many years ago and talk about how the baby's badly decomposed body was found in the woods near the house from where he'd been taken.

They ignore me as I sit quietly in the corner, shivering in secret, and soaking up every word.

Chapter Twelve

Baby Jerry

"Mama. Mama. Maaa Maaa!" My terrified screams reach to her downstairs bedroom. It's pitch black in my room. Something alive is in here with me. It's swishing around the room. I keep screaming until I hear her on the creaky steps.

"What?" she says sleepily.

"There's somebody in here."

"No, there's not." She looks under the bed and in the closet. "There's nothing here to hurt you. Go back to sleep."

She doesn't know what I know — that my room swirls with shadowy figures that say horrible things to me that I can't talk about.

Your daddy's going to kill you with a knife, the voice says to me, along with *Na, na, nobody loves you, you're ugly.*

Mama pulls the covers up around my chin and leaves. I shiver and shake and hide my head under my pillow. Something laughs.

I wake up terrified every night so my calls for Mama are a regular middle-of-the-night thing. The voice urges me to say those filthy words I hear from Daddy sometimes. I resist, resist, resist, until finally I just give in and say them all. And then it sort of hushes and leaves me alone for a while.

Night after night, I lie awake, every sense tuned to what is going on downstairs. If I hear the knife drawer in the kitchen open, I hold my breath until I can't hold it any longer and wait—and wait—in breathless terror for Daddy's footsteps on the stairs.

When he responds to my screams it's with a hug and a whisper of, "You're okay, honey, nothing is going to get you. I won't let it."

Usually though, it's Mama who comes up. "Stop it. You're too big for this. Have a little faith."

Faith? Faith? In what?

"Go back to sleep you're just fine."

One afternoon Mama says, "Would it be alright if I put Bernie in bed with you? We're going to need his crib for Jerry."

I sleep better with Bernie's warm, snugly roly-poly body next to mine. I no longer scream in the night for fear of waking him up. But I keep watch, checking the closet, looking under the bed. The voices are still in my head but I don't see anything.

§

It's a hot August day. Aunt Helen invites us to her house for dinner after church. It's late afternoon when we drive in our own driveway, tired and hot. There in the barnyard are seven big fat hogs that look dead.

My dad's "Ohhh," is one of pure pain, and the tears flow down his cheeks as he pounds the steering wheel.

130

He holds his head in his hands. "I knew I should have come home. I knew I should have come home."

This is the first time I have ever seen my daddy cry. "God, oh my God, why? Why? Why did you do this to me?" Daddy's broken voice sucks me in until I feel I am inside his gut feeling his despair.

Daddy didn't say it, but it was like I heard it anyway: *This is your fault, Edith. I went to your sister's house to please you and now look what's happened.* No, he didn't say that, but I heard it.

"Heat exhaustion," he says. "The windmill didn't blow enough to put water in the tank. This is our whole livelihood. This is the only money we have coming in this fall."

Mama hustles the little kids upstairs, saying, "Let's change your clothes," leaving Daddy in his agony.

I want to do something for him, but there is nothing I can do that can keep him from blaming himself. I put my arms around his neck.

"God is punishing me," he says in a weak and hopeless voice. His hat is on the floor where it fell when we walked in. His black hair is matted with sweat and his shirt is wet and sticking to him. "Oh God! Oh God! Oh God! What am I going to do?"

That does it for me and God. I already don't like him much. I know God has the power to destroy us. That's even more clear to me than it was when I saw a movie in church of Him ordering Abraham to offer his own son as a living sacrifice. Abraham is standing over his son who is tied to pile of wood, with a knife ready to plunge it into his heart. I can't get that picture out of my mind. *Who does God think he is?*

§

A few hot days before school starts, the sky grows scary black and still and the dust starts swirling around. After evening chores, as Daddy and Ted run for the house, milk sloshes from the swinging milk buckets onto the baked dry soil. Ted has more on his clothes than is left in the pail when he reaches the house. Sticky sweet milk mixes with the mud on their clothes in strange patterns.

All of us huddle in the kitchen listening to the wind, watching through the window as the hog barn explodes, the chicken coop splinters and splatters, and chickens fly everywhere. They squawk helplessly as they blow out of sight or hit the side of buildings and fall dead on the ground. A shed on the end of the barn turns into a pile of splinters. When the wind stops, we race around barefoot in the mud, trying to rescue chickens.

I step on a board with a nail in it and hobble to the house. Mama gets a pan of hot water, puts some Epson salts in it and makes me sit and soak my foot, while she makes a bread and milk poultice to slap on the nail hole in my heel. I have to stay in the house. I hate being kept in while everyone else is out playing in the mud.

"You shouldn't have been out there anyway," Daddy says when he sees my foot. "You're a girl."

First the hogs, then the chickens. What's next, God?

What's next is Belle. She lies down on a pitchfork. The vet comes and gives her a shot. "I don't know if this will save her," he says to Mama. Mama brings hot water to the barn and Ted puts it on her wounds. Mama even makes Belle a bread and milk poultice, but nothing saves her. We kids are crying. There's nothing we can do— we're helpless.

§

Caring for another baby is a pain in the neck. There are more diapers to wash, and Jerry is sick all the time. Mama and Daddy have to drive him over a hundred miles to see a doctor once a week so they are always gone. When they are home, the baby needs his nose flushed out, his lungs aspirated, and his medicine measured just so.

"Here, feed the baby," Mama says, handing me a bottle. I feel guilty for not wanting to help take care of him.

I don't want to feed the baby. Mama is always asking me to help. "Bubbles, go get me a diaper. Bubbles, can you pick up the baby? My hands are dirty. Go see what Bernie's doing, peel some potatoes, put some water on to boil, set the table, run upstairs and get me some clean clothes. Bill's been in the mud again."

Daddy is working day and night as he's taken a job as a hired man for old Mr. Barnes. On our farm he's plowing under stubble, planting winter wheat, harvesting corn, and putting up hay.

I look out my window and see the lights of his tractor going around and around in the field at night. Sometimes I see him come in at dawn, dog-tired and dirty. He washes up, gets some hot coffee and breakfast, and then goes to work for Mr. Barnes.

"You're the man of the family when I'm not here," Daddy says to Ted. "Make sure the cows get milked and the hogs and chickens get fed. And don't forget to put Bessie in the other pasture away from the bull."

Mama is starting to make Daddy take Ted with him whenever he goes to town. It's much more peaceful when he's not around, but I'm jealous.

"Why does Ted always get to go with Daddy? Why don't I ever get to go?"

"I need you here." Mama's voice is firm.

§

Christmas! Excitement is in the air in spite of all the chaos. Colorful Christmas catalogues from Sears and Montgomery Ward come in the mail. We turn the pages of the catalogues for hours, making lists of everything we want Santa to bring.

A scraggly pine tree sits in our living room covered with the usual strings of popcorn and cranberries, stars made from cookie dough, popsicle stick crèches made in Sunday school, and colored macaroni pasted on construction paper that we worked hard on at the kitchen table on Sunday afternoons.

Under the tree are homemade gifts we made with love in school for Mama and Daddy, carefully wrapped in Christmas paper brought to school by our teacher.

"By golly," Daddy says, "that sure is a pretty tree."

"That's an ugly tree," Ted spits out sourly to me. "Dad's just sayin' that." I remember Aunt Dorothy's trees and silently agree with him.

The Christmas program is scheduled for the last Friday before Christmas. We've been practicing for weeks and I have a solo to sing. I can't wait for Mama and Daddy to hear me sing *Away In A Manger*. There's only eleven of us in school, and everyone has parts to perform in the play and pieces to say. I don't know if I'm more excited about the big production or that school's going to be closed for two weeks.

Days before the program, I'm thrilled and excited as I get to go to Aberdeen with Mama and Daddy when they take Jerry to the doctor. I told the teacher yesterday afternoon and did my schoolwork ahead of time.

After breakfast I'm waiting to go when Mama says, "Get to school."

"You said I could go with you."

"No, you can't. I need you here to take care of the boys."

I sob out, "You said I could go if my schoolwork was all done. Please, please, you said I could."

Did she really say I could go or did I just make it up in my head?

Mama is wrapping Jerry in a blanket while Daddy is carrying the diaper bag to the car.

I stumble in the direction of our schoolhouse as Mama and Daddy roar down the dirt road, leaving me down in the ditch eating their dust.

My teacher is extra kind to me when I show up late with swollen, tear-stained eyes. "Are you okay?" she asks.

Hiding my face from her I say, "Just fine, thank you."

It's been dark for a while. Aunt Dorothy stops in and checks to see if we need anything.
"You guys okay?" she asks. "Got enough wood for the fire?" She throws on a few logs and says, "They will be home soon. Don't light any matches to light the lamps until they get home."

Ted does the chores, while I make peanut butter sandwiches for all of us. Then we play games in the half dark until we see headlights in the drive.

Daddy carries Jerry in and lays him tenderly in his basket. Mama has her arms full of packages that she takes to her room and throws on the bed. After they light the lamps and settle in, Mama hands me a package with a pink satin blouse and a navy-blue skirt, made of yards and yards of taffeta to wear in the school Christmas program. There are some black suede shoes to go with it.

Thrilled to my bones, I hold my bounty close to my chest. "Oh, thank you, thank you, Mama. I love this—all of it!"

"Now aren't you ashamed of your behavior?" she tosses back at me.

Humiliated, I feel like throwing my new clothes and shoes at her, but I go upstairs with my loot.

§

The day of the Christmas program starts out snowy. It's freezing cold. The prairie wind howls outside. School gets out at two instead of the usual four o'clock. Ted and Mike milk the cows early and bring in pails of warm frothy milk.

There is excitement in the air! We eat early, full of enthusiasm and eager to get dressed for the Christmas program. Our teacher says Santa is going to be there to bring candy and presents. Daddy isn't home. His food is warming on the stove. We are picking up our dishes when Mama walks fast to the phone and calls the bar for Daddy.

"Is Lon Jones there?"

Her voice is strange, as if she is strangling and forcing the words out. She waits. Her face is gray.

What's wrong? There must be something terribly wrong.

"Get home now. Right now."

I've never heard her talk to him like that. She's never even called him at the bar before, that I know of. I walk in the living room and look in Jerry's basket. He is lying very still, not breathing his usual raspy breaths. I touch his face and it's stone cold and stiff.

"Don't touch him, go wash up, and get ready for the program." Mama's frosty voice, sends a chill up my spine.

I put on my new clothes and shoes and help the boys with their shirts and ties.

Daddy walks in the house with two huge brown paper bags of groceries. He doesn't even get in the door before Mama says, "Jerry's dead." Cans and boxes tumble to the floor, macaroni spills all over when the bag breaks and cans roll everywhere under the stove and under the table.

"Ohhh," Daddy groans and he staggers against the doorjamb.

I drop to the floor in my new clothes and start picking up groceries. The boys grab cans and boxes and pile them on the table. Mama runs for her coat while Daddy grabs Jerry and wraps him in a blanket. Somebody puts Bernie's coat on him.

"We have to leave," Mama says. On their way out the door into the frosty night, Mama throws these words at us: "You kids go be in the play; they can't have it without you."

We put on our coats, gloves, mittens, caps, and overshoes, blow out the kerosene lamps, and scamper wordlessly down the moonlit road. The cold wind stings our cheeks, and tries to force us off the road into the ditch. I hang on to Ted, Mike and Bill hang on to me. The bitter cold makes our noses run and brings tears to our eyes. We struggle through the icy air until we get to the schoolhouse door. Once inside, the schoolroom is warm and inviting and full of people staring at us.

Our teacher has been anxiously waiting and is unhappy. "Where have you been? Hurry up, you're late. Go get your costumes on."

Behind the sheets pinned to a wire to make curtains, I whisper to our teacher, "I think my little brother is dead."

"Why are you lying to me? You wouldn't be here if that was true," she hisses.

The program begins, we say our lines, and I sing my solo with my stomach in knots, looking around the room for my parents. *They aren't here.* Santa comes bringing gifts and candy in brown paper bags—and the adults are laughing and talking. I'm dreading the thought of walking back to our dark, sad house.

Our teacher stands up, claps her hands for attention and announces, "I want to give a special thank-you to the Jones kids for showing up tonight in spite of the tragedy at their house." A slow murmur starts and gets louder and just like that the party is over.

Somebody drives us home. Other neighbors come behind us. The house is full of people when my parents walk in—without Jerry.

Where is he? I don't dare ask. We go to bed and fall asleep to the soft murmur of voices downstairs.

The next couple of days are a flurry of visitors. The kitchen counters and tables are piled high with hams, pot roasts, casseroles, cakes and pies, brought by aunts, uncles, friends, and neighbors. They come to the door with sympathy and arms loaded, then they sit around in the living room where the casket is.

I look in the casket when they bring it in and see Jerry lying there in a white romper suit—his tiny little feet wearing white leather shoes and a white satin blanket covering part of him. He lies there in a blue stillness as everyone talks in hushed tones. We tiptoe around wanting to help—and wanting to stay out of the way— and wanting this nightmare to end.

§

Christmas Eve morning we sit sadly at the breakfast table, half-heartedly eating something from the stacks of food on the counter. The howling wind blows the freezing snow, and spits the swirling white ice kernels against the frosty windowpanes. Mama is in her bedroom, getting ready for the funeral. Daddy is out in the barn doing chores. Somebody I don't know is helping him. I see the man bring two pails of milk to the back porch and set them inside the door. A woman pours them into our tall black separator on the porch and starts to crank the handle.

Mama comes out to the kitchen dressed in her good black dress, her face pale and looking so very tired. In a quiet voice she says, "Go get your good clothes on kids. Bubbles, it's really cold out there. Wear a pair of jeans under your dress. You can take them off inside the church."

Two strange men in dark suits with white shirts and dark ties walk in, the swirling snow riding in on their shoulders. They stomp their feet and brush the snow from their hair. In the living room they pick up the casket, maneuver it around the corner, and carefully take it out the back door. They tell Mama they'll see her at the church and put the casket in a long black car.

We follow them in our car. Nobody pushes or shoves or argues—it's as if we're all dead. At the church, I run to the church basement and take off the jeans under my dress. Mama follows me down there and puts on her black felt hat with the black veil.

Then we join Daddy in the hallway and wait for our walk down the aisle to the front row. The boys are lined up beside Daddy. Mama is statue-still and steel-quiet. She holds my hand. We all sit staring at the white closed casket, listening to Mrs. Peterson play the piano while some high school girls sing *Beyond The Sunset*.

I'm crying too hard to hear what the minister is saying. Mama has no tears. She hands me her white handkerchief to dry my tear-filled eyes. *Is Jerry really dead and never coming back? It's my fault. I didn't want to hold him. I was tired of feeding him and washing his diapers.* Guilt fills me and takes up a home in my stomach.

Midnight Christmas Eve service finds us sitting in church dressed in our finest, like any other Christmas Eve, listening to Mama sing her Christmas solo. It's been a long day. Mama's family and some neighbors came home with us after the funeral and only left when it was time for them to do chores.

Before we left for church, we hung up a peculiar mixture of stockings for Santa to fill. Mike always wants to use one of Daddy's because it's way bigger than his.

He'd use Mama's nylon stocking if she'd let him. I'm disappointed to see the stockings still empty and the cookies by the tree untouched when we get home.

Mama is exhausted. "You kids go to bed. Dad will light the way and hear your prayers tonight." All five of us huddle together in the one double bed in the boy's room, too excited to sleep. We take turns running to the long window to see if we can catch Santa. We have firm orders not to come downstairs before 6:00 am. We lie awake and whisper to each other, until one by one we fall asleep.

But Christmas morning our excitement is gone. Santa put something in the stockings before morning but the usual squeals of "Look, look what I got" are missing. Daddy loads the potbellied stove with coal, stirring the fire with his poker and we all sit on the floor by the tree and open gifts. Every time Mama comes across something for Jerry, she sets it aside. Later she and I open them.

Aunt Helen and her family plow through snowdrifts to get to our house for dinner. There are mountains of food still sitting on the porch. My girl cousins are quiet. They cry when they see the empty baby basket. I try to laugh in all the right places and do what I'm told. I'm so afraid of hurting Mama's feelings if I cry—or do what I feel like doing, which is hit something.

In bed I lie awake talking to God and I say all the nasty words I've ever heard Daddy say. I curse God for taking my baby brother and then beg him to bring Jerry back to life. I promise I would never complain again about having to take care of him. I promise I would do anything God wants if he will just bring Jerry back. "You brought Lazarus back to life, why can't you bring Jerry back to life?"

But God is silent. Daddy's words eat at my gut like a cancer: "If you fight with your brothers, God will come and take one of them away,"

Furiously sucking my thumb doesn't comfort me. Rolling from side to side in my tangled blankets, I am so sad and sorry that it feels like it's eating me alive. *I am guilty, guilty, guilty.* I suddenly know, without a doubt, how much power God has. A person can be there one minute and gone the next and there is nothing anyone can do about it. God could easily take me too. He could just strike me dead with no warning. *He probably will right now.*

Night after night I beg God, trying to sob quietly so I won't wake Bernie. The pillow I'm burying my face in is wet with my sniffling and snuffling when Mama comes upstairs.

"What's the matter?"

"I'm afraid I'm going to die like Jerry." I don't tell Mama but I am also thinking, *Jerry never did anything wrong, but I am the brat who does nothing but cause trouble . . . and now God took Jerry to punish me.*

"Don't be silly."

I sob harder. Mama touches my back. "Come downstairs and sleep on the couch." In the cold, dark living room, huddled under a blanket, I flop first one way and then the other. I can't stop thinking about Jerry

143

and how awful I am. Finally, Mama comes out and lies down on the couch, fitting like a spoon next to me. She slings one arm over my waist and I go to sleep inside the cocoon of her body.

§

In the deep snow months, we play cards, checkers, marbles, Canasta, Whist, and Pinochle. Any kid who can recognize a heart from a spade learns to play. If the snow is too deep to go to school, we play all day long. We make fudge and cookies and popcorn balls and eat a lot of pancakes. The only sounds are bantering, bragging, and giggles.

Because we have to preserve the clear glass tubes that bring power to our brown, table-high short-wave radio, we only turn it on twice a day—once to hear the noon news, then again to listen to the evening weather report.

The windows are full of thick frost. We take a knife or a razor blade and scrape at it to make a big hole so we can see the spiraling snow as it gets deeper and deeper. I know what Mama says is true: "We are so lucky to have a nice warm house and food to eat."

I wonder, *Is winter ever going to get over*? At least Daddy doesn't go to town much when the roads are drifted shut with snow. Still, once in a while, he hitches up the team and drives the wagon to town to get groceries.

Chapter Thirteen

The Mystery Man

I'm standing at the well pumping a pail of water. It's really hot out here even for July. I see a sleek black car slowly driving down the dirt road and turn right into our driveway. Leaving the water at the well, I run to grab our old yellow dog, Buff, who's barking furiously. "He won't hurt you," I yell and watch as what seems like a seven-foot man unwinds out of the car. He reaches back into the car for his straw hat, rolls up the sleeves on his crisp cotton shirt, and starts toward our door. He is wearing overalls that don't look like they've ever gotten dirty or even been washed yet.

Daddy comes from the barn to greet him. "Come on in, could you use a sandwich or a cup of coffee?"

"Sure can. Do you have time to talk?"

Later I hear Daddy tell Mama that Aldren is looking for a job. He doesn't want money, just a place to sleep and food to eat.

"God is good," Mama says.

"He's a strange one," Daddy tells Mama after Aldren has been here for a few days. "He's a good hand and does what I tell him to do, but he's not a farmer. His hands are clean and soft and I have to explain everything. But it doesn't take too many brains to feed the hogs and he knows how to muck out a stall."

Every night when supper is over, Mama and I do the dishes in a chipped white enamel pan after heating water in it on the cookstove. Aldren sits at the kitchen table and works on papers that he digs out of a bulging, brown-leather briefcase. I watch him rifle through the briefcase and get out a sharp pencil, or an ink bottle and a quill pen.

Mama tells me she'd sure like to go in his room and see what's in that briefcase. Aldren won't even let her change the sheets or make the bed in his room, which was my room. More than once he's said, "I'll do it myself, Edith, you have enough to do."

Sometimes on Sunday afternoons we all climb into his long black car and ride around the countryside. The car slowly crawls down the dusty road from crop to crop, inspecting the wheat, the oats, the corn, the beans, as we drive past the other farms we wav out the window at whoever is outside.

"Who lives there? Aldren asks.

"That's the Weavers, over there's the Smiths, and that's the Lawrence farm," Daddy tells him. Then he shares whatever tidbits of information he has about each of these farmers.

"Do you suppose Aldren is spying on somebody?" Daddy asks Mama.

"Why don't you ask him?"

"No, I don't think I want to know. Besides it's none of our business."

On an August Sunday, Aldren drives off and doesn't come back. When he isn't there for chores Monday morning, Daddy says, "Maybe he isn't coming back."

Late in the afternoon we're amazed as a red-and-white Piper Cub plane circles our farmhouse, lands in the pasture across the road, and slowly glides to a stop. We watch as the propeller on the airplane goes from furiously fast to slow and finally stops.

The boys and I stand there stiff with excitement. Mama comes out of the house shading her eyes. Aldren climbs out of the airplane dressed in a leather bombardier jacket, a leather hat, glossy brown trousers, and a tan shirt. He is carrying his precious briefcase under his arm. He stands by the barbwire stock gate scanning the dirt road to the south as a car drives up. He waves to us, climbs in the car, and zooms off leaving a cloud of dust and five stunned people in his wake.

Aldren comes back after supper with no explanation. I am curious, but we all know better than to ask adults questions. The next evening and the next and the next, we get to zoom through the air in the Piper Cub, all of us kids except Bernie. We ride two at a time, twisting and turning, soaring through the sky, sometimes flying upside down. The thrill makes my throbbing heart nearly jump out of my chest with excitement. Some evenings we just glide around over the other farms.

"He's spying on somebody," I hear my Daddy say one night.

"I sure wonder who he really is," Mama says.

"Well, he works hard so I guess that's all that counts."

Daddy's curious, but doesn't seem really concerned. I wonder, *Does Daddy know more than he's telling Mama? Maybe he has to keep it a secret! Or does he really just like the guy?*

Aldren seems to be a great person. He's fun, he brings Tootsie Rolls, horehound candy sticks, and Butterfinger bars, and he does lots of chores. I don't know and I don't care if he's spying on somebody from the air. It's all so exciting.

"Come on, go for a ride in the plane. It's safe." Aldren is trying to coax Mama and Daddy.

Mama says, "I'm too busy."

Daddy says, "No, I'm not getting in that thing."

Ted and I side with Aldren. "Oh, come on Daddy, it's fun. If we can do it, you can do it."

Aldren says he'll be leaving in a few days and this is Daddy's last chance to go for a ride.

Saturday morning Daddy bravely says, "I guess if my kids can do it I can."

All of us stand out in the field watching as he climbs into the passenger seat, looking like he doesn't want to. The propeller slowly comes alive, the plane taxis to the end of the field, turns around, heads in our direction, lifts off, and oh no—it crashes!

Daddy gets out holding his head, Aldren crawls out the other side and says, "That wind is stronger than I thought it was." The propeller on the plane is broken.

Aldren stashes the pieces in the trunk of his car and leaves.

A week later he comes back with a new propeller and someone to fix his plane. When it is fixed he shakes Daddy's hand, hands Mama an envelope, tells us, "Be good kids," and flies off.

"Maybe he's IRS?" Daddy says. "Maybe government business. Maybe the FBI? Maybe even the mob? He did look sort of Italian, didn't he?"

§

Daddy and Ted go to town a lot in the rattling old pick-up. Sometimes they don't come home until way after dark.

My handsome older brother, whom I adore, is even meaner and harder to get along with than ever. He makes it hard for me to want to be loyal to him.

"What do you do all that time you're gone?" I ask.

"Oh, eat, play games, make Dad come home."

"That doesn't sound like fun."

"Well, sometimes there's some other kids around . . . and the women in the bar like me a lot. In fact—I've learned a lot from them."

"What?"

"You wouldn't understand."

"What wouldn't I understand?"

"Doing it."

"What's *it*?"

"If I told you, you wouldn't understand. Mom and Dad do it in the middle of the night when we're supposed to be asleep. I've heard them through the transom."

Ted does stuff to the girls I bring home to stay a day or two with me. Lois and Donna and Norma all tell me about him touching them and trying to show them things. I've been sort of curious about what goes on up in that haymow. Why would they want to be with him instead of me. I guess it's not a big deal.

§

Daddy sells the livestock, so we have money to visit Grandma Jones. "I want my mother to see all my kids before it's too late," he says. We pile suitcases in the old gray Dodge with the dusty seats, and leave for Missouri to visit Grandmother Minnie.

It's our first trip anywhere since we moved to the farm. I hadn't seen Grandma since that time in Custer when she was too busy to notice me. I'm excited to miss three weeks of school.

We're in the car when old Weaver drives in. "Don't worry Lon, I'll take care of the place while you're gone." Then he stands, a tired old man in ragged clothes, watching as he pulls out of the driveway past the mounds of hard snow piled high in the yard. The howling March winds seem to push us down the road.

"Bye-bye school," Mike and Bill shout at the quiet building that is nearly empty without the four of us.

"Good thing we're leaving now. There's another blizzard coming," Daddy says. "It'll be nice and warm in Missouri. Hell, Ella's got her garden in already."

The first couple of hours go pretty well. Mama hands out crackers and baloney, oatmeal cookies, and roast beef sandwiches. Then it starts, first the kids, then Mama.

"How much longer?"

"Color some pictures."

"We've already done that."

"Take a nap."

"Too much racket."

"How about you play road bingo. Find signs with all the letters in the word Bingo and nobody can use the same sign. The first person to see it, gets it."

We stop for gas and to use the outhouse. Daddy fills the water bag in case the radiator needs water when we're out in the middle of nowhere. Riding in the car is getting really old. We read funny books, Mama sings us songs, Daddy tells us jokes, and finally at dark we are someplace in Iowa. We check into a tall brick hotel with shadowy, musty hallways that smells like lemon oil and ground-in dirt.

In through the heavy wooden door that opens to our room we go carrying sacks, suitcases, blankets, and pillows. Daddy takes off to explore and find some food. Mama quickly locks the door. "Don't any of you kids unlock this door for any reason."

Is she scared? She looks scared.

151

Daddy comes back with bread and more baloney, pop, and chips. Mama opens a jar of pickles. She and Daddy and Bernie have the bed; the rest of us sleep on the floor. Early the next morning we hit the road again.

We finally get to Grandma's. She's even more pint-sized, withered, and bent over now. She looks like a sack of rags with her long, long black hair and tiny bird face peeking out of clothes that are too big for her.

Grandma lives in a small, faded and weathered brown cottage that Daddy bought for her when she no longer had anyone to live with on the farm. She smiles happily but weakly when she sees us and sits up a little straighter in her rocking chair. Grandma is so frail that we can't hug her or even get too close. With a small smile she feebly shakes each of our hands. I am sort of in awe as we greet Grandma quietly.

We're all remembering what Daddy said when he pulled the car over for a last bathroom break just outside of town: "You kids remember your manners." We can all recite his rules by heart. "Stand up straight, square your shoulders, don't slouch, sit up in that chair, don't put your elbows on the table, don't reach for food, ask to have it passed, don't lick your knife like old Weaver, don't talk with your mouth full, eat with your mouth closed, don't speak unless spoken to, and never tell anyone who doesn't live in our house what goes on in our house. I'm not raising a bunch of ill-mannered brats."

Waiting for us at Aunt Ella's house are cousins and relatives, so many of them the living room is full and we spill out onto the porch. Wow is it warm out. The southern foods that Daddy loves are everywhere — hominy grits, black-eyed peas, fried potatoes, biscuits, side pork, hams, fried chicken, apple and peach pies, all piled high on the tables and the sideboards. We're all over the house and out in the yard eating and drinking tea and soda. The March cold and snow of South Dakota seems far away.

The town where they live is small, with no sidewalks or cafes, but there is an old general store made of logs where daddy buys his cigarettes and we get bubblegum for a penny. The storeowner recognizes Daddy and pumps his hand up and down, asking questions like, "When'd ya'all get to town? How long youse stayen?"

We snicker at the word *youse*. Mama always corrects us. "Say you — it's not youse." In fact, we can hardly get through a sentence without Mama correcting our English.

After a couple of days we drive out of Missouri and wind high up in the hills of Arkansas, driving on gravel roads through thick trees. We're going to see Daddy's old "stompin' grounds" and meet some more relatives. Eyes wide, stomach in my throat, I watch as we drive on a narrow rocky road through woods and near deep streams. We stop at a cotton plantation and visit with the Negro folks working in the fields. I've never seen a Negro person before, and I am fascinated by their speech and their hair.

We eat in a restaurant owned by a Negro family, with several kids just about our age. The woman waits on us

153

and her husband cooks us side pork, cornbread, and beans, after which Mama takes pictures of their whole family with us lined up in front of them.

Finally, we reach the backwoods of Arkansas. There high on a mountain we surprise Daddy's cousin Will, who seems overjoyed to see us. He pumps Daddy's hand. "Come in, come in." The noisy buzz of talk and laughter goes on and on. Piles of fried potatoes, grits, beans, dandelion greens, biscuits, gravy, sweet potatoes, catfish fried in cornmeal, jams, jellies, and pies, just keep coming.

We sleep on the porch under homemade quilts for a couple of nights. Daddy and Will go hunting and bring home rabbits and squirrel to eat. We watch as Emma fries them up for supper. Mamma takes a mass of pictures on her Brownie camera using up all her rolls of film and then it's time to go.

Will and his big family stand in the gravel patch that is his driveway and wave until we can't see them anymore.

"Did you notice," Mama says to no one in particular, "everybody is fat." It's true, all the relatives in Missouri and Arkansas are fat.

There are two things you can't be if you live in our house: one is fat and the other is Catholic.

We go back to Grandma's house for a couple days and finally back to South Dakota and school.

Grandma dies a few weeks later. The call comes about nine o'clock one night. Mama answers the phone and I hear her say, "I'm so sorry. I'll tell him when he comes home. I'm sure he'll be there as soon as he can. Take care of yourself, Ella."

I stand in our driveway the next morning, on a bright May day, dressed in my skirt and sweater for school. I watch Daddy leave and pieces of me go with him. I hate it when he's not here. One good thing about it though, Mama lets me and Bernie sleep with her. It's a lot closer to the outhouse from her bedroom than it is from mine.

Chapter Fourteen

Family

Just about suppertime one evening, I answer a knock
on our door to find a tall, lanky, good-looking guy
wearing a dusty black cowboy hat standing there. With
him is a little, round dark-haired woman with laughing
eyes and a thick mop of brown hair.

"Does Lon Jones live here?" the man in jeans and a
checkered shirt asks.

By now Daddy's at the door behind me. "Chuck!" he
bellows. "What are you doing here?"

"Came to see you. This is my wife Jean."

"Come in, come in." Smiling and turning to Mama,
Daddy says, "Edith, this is my cousin Chuck from
Arkansas."

While Daddy and his company are talking at the
table, Mama slips out to kill a chicken. "Go to the cellar
and get a jar of green beans, and one of tomatoes," she
tells me.

Jean talks in a sweet southern drawl and she is
wearing shorts—*shorts! Married women don't wear shorts—
do they?* They're driving a rickety, beat up black pick-up.

One fried chicken dinner later, when Jean and Chuck
go to the outhouse, Daddy pulls me and Ted aside.

"Be nice to them, they're homeless. Chuck's been in
the war and he's shell-shocked so don't make any

sudden loud noises around him." It isn't the first time
I've heard of someone being shell-shocked. Daddy's said
this before about men who've come to our house to help
with chores or for a meal.

It's easy to be nice to Chuck. He's full of southern
charm and treats me and Mama with great respect.
During the war he'd been in France and he speaks to me
in French. Jean translates some of it to mean "you're a
pretty girl and you have great posture."

By the end of the summer I love him—and like Jean a
lot. He calls me sweetheart and teaches me a few French
words. Chuck works in the field, helps Ted with the
chores, and goes to town with Daddy.

Jean helps me and Mike churn butter, and wash the
glass chimneys for the kerosene lamps. She giggles and
chirps as she helps with the cooking, the gardening, the
floor scrubbing, and watches the kids so Mama can go do
her church things.

There's enough work for all of us: chickens to feed,
eggs to collect, milk to strain and separate in the big iron
separator, cream to pour into a big tin cream can in the
cool cellar so it can be sold to the creamery on Saturday
night. There is laundry to do, sheets to be changed every
week, water to carry from the well, ironing, and always
the never-ending cooking and dishes to wash. I really
like having Jean here.

Chuck watches Daddy make fun of me and put me
down when he is in one of his moods. Because of a thing
called hay fever, I am always wiping my swollen itchy
eyes, blowing my runny nose, putting cold washcloths

on my swollen face, and wishing for a freeze. Every August it bothers me.

Daddy thinks I am sneering at him, wrinkling my nose at him on purpose. "Stop wrinkling your nose at me," he says in a gruff voice.

"I'm not."

"Yes, you are; now stop it."

When he and Chuck get home from town, Daddy sits around and pokes at me with his words while I wash the supper dishes. Things like, "You don't like me much," or "You're ashamed of me." Or "Chuck did you ever see a bigger tomboy or anybody more scatterbrained?"

I don't dare answer Daddy back. Pretending not to care when he jabs at me, I smile at Chuck, and that makes Daddy even madder.

"You're a rotten, spoiled, ungrateful kid. A flighty, reckless, snotty brat, too good for me. You act just like your aunt Ruth. Make sure that dish is clean."

Why is Daddy saying this? Is he crazy? Why is he slurring his words? Did he stagger? No, it must be my imagination.

When I see the sympathy in Chuck's eyes I feel so low. I hate sympathy. Mama says women who cry are weak and pathetic.

As soon as the dishes are done, I go off by myself to cry and lick my wounds in the wrecked car in the backyard—my secret and alone place.

At breakfast Daddy says, "There's my sweetheart." *Is he nuts?*

When the first snow comes, Chuck says, "This is not for me. Guess we'll go to Arizona and see if we can find work there." They hug us all good-bye.

"Want to come with us?" Chuck asks me. I know they're teasing, but part of me longs to go with them, and part of me knows I'd die away from my family.

Chapter Fifteen

Don't Tell

It's a crisp clear, cold, sunny, perfectly still, spring Saturday—or at least it was earlier when I made my usual trip to the outhouse. There is no school so I go back to bed and snuggle back under my pile of soft warm quilts for a while. But hunger drives me downstairs. Mama is nowhere to be seen. Daddy is standing out in the driveway staring down the road. Maybe he knows where Mama is.

"Who ya watching for?"

"I'm waiting for the doctor. Your mother's in trouble." The concern in his eyes as he answers warns me, but I ask anyway.

"What kind of trouble?"

He brushes me off.

"Don't bother me. I can't talk right now."

A car wheels fast into our driveway, a man jumps out, grabs a black bag, and sprints for the house. Daddy ushers him through the door and I follow them in. Bill and Bernie come sleepy-eyed down the steps. Ted and Mike come in with pails of milk, pour them in the separator in the porch and ask, "Where's Mama?"

"In the bedroom with Daddy and the doctor."

"Why?"

"I don't know."

Daddy comes out for a teakettle full of hot water and the dishpan. He's too busy to look our way.

We sit around the table scared, quietly eating cereal. The bedroom door off the kitchen opens and the doctor comes out with towels smeared with blood on his arm. He's carrying the white enamel dish pan full of bloody water and something. We watch him, our eyes big, as he goes to the door.

"Where's your outhouse?" We all point and answer together "Back there."

He comes back with an empty pan and no bloody towels. He rolls down his sleeves, shakes my Daddy's hand and leaves.

Daddy makes Mama some breakfast and says, "Bubbles, keep the kids quiet. Mama needs to rest."

Hours later, Mama gets up and makes supper.

"What's wrong, Mama? We're scared."

"Nothing, I'm just fine."

"Are you sick?"

"No, I'm fine."

She doesn't look fine. Daddy is rushing around trying to help her instead of telling me to do it.

Then I overhear her ask Daddy in a low voice, "Could he tell if it was a boy or a girl?"

§

"Ally-Oop do you think you could drive Doc's little Ford tractor around the field and do some planting for him?" Daddy asks.

Ted puffs out his chest, "Yeah, I've driven it a couple times."

"Doc has a propane gas refrigerator he's offered to sell me for sixty dollars. He needs a hand for summer. He'll pay you three dollars a day so mom can have the refrigerator. And you can earn some money for school clothes too."

Ted squares his shoulders, looks at Dad and says, "Yeah, Dad, I can do it." Ted is twelve now.

"I'll be south of town working for old Mr. Barnes, I'll be counting on you kids to take care of your mother and keep things going."

"Okay, Dad."

I hate that Daddy has to work for Mr. Barnes. I've heard people say he's mean. Once we heard he killed a cow with a cow stool.

"Do you have to go there?" I ask.

"Yep, we need the money. Gotta feed you kids." He says this with a sigh that makes me wish we weren't such a burden.

From our yard I see the tractor Ted's driving go around and around from one end of the field to another, the heat shimmering through big clouds of dust. Ted comes in for supper late at night sunburned and very tired.

Mrs. Harmon, who owns a cafe in town, asks Mama if I can babysit for her three little kids, all day, every day. I pack up a suitcase because I have to stay all night so I'll be there early in the mornings when the two little girls get up. By the end of day three I know I can't do it. I call home. "Mama," I whisper on the phone, so no one hears me, "please come get me. I hate it here."

Mama comes and apologizes and says, "Maybe she's just too young for this job."

§

I am growing breasts and don't want to be called Bubbles anymore. I announce to everyone that I will no longer answer to Bubbles. I correct everyone who says it. "My name is Evelyn," I say as politely as I can to Sunday school teachers and store clerks. Only Aunt Dorothy refuses to change. Because I love her, I let her keep on doing it.

Mama has boxes of dusty, shabby old books in our upstairs closet. My hungry eyes feast on them every chance I get. In them I learn about romance. Women wait for men to notice them; they play stupid, silly games to get a man's attention. The hero and the heroines suffer from love that isn't returned and messages that go astray. Lovers never tell each other what they're doing or thinking. I even read where sometimes a man may spank his woman to make her mind. *For darn sure, no man is ever going to spank me and live to tell the story.*

The stories fill up my desperate need to be loved. It feels like my whole body leans into these books. I think about dashing, handsome, "swashbuckling" men who sweep women off their feet. I read with longing the stories about hot desire, forbidden impulses, passions, and heroes mad about beautiful damsels. It's so much easier to live in that crazy, make-believe world than to live in what my bare-boned life is really like.

While I'm strangely drawn to the books, I can't figure out why people don't just tell each other what's on their minds. I talk back to the text. "Go tell her how you feel, you idiot. Stop waiting for him to read your mind, you dimwitted ninny."

Somebody brings some *Good Housekeeping* magazines to our house and I find a picture of the perfect girl's bedroom. I want a room like this so bad! I find Mama and show her the picture of the white eyelet canopy bed with white satin quilts, a window seat with velvet cushions, and fluffy, lacy pink dolls sitting on white dressers with gold drawer handles.

She takes a look and sniffs. "It wouldn't look like this if you had it. Your room is always a mess, clothes laying everywhere."

Crushed, I throw the magazine down and head blindly for the door. *No use telling her anything — ever.*

§

Hot and dirty, Ted staggers in the house one afternoon. His face and shirtless body are bright red and this time it's not sunburn. "Measles!" "Mama exclaims. "Why did you stay in the field for so long?" She helps him upstairs to bed. I follow with a pan of water and towels.

Ted lies in the hot bedroom for days with wet washcloths on his swollen-shut eyes. Burning up with fever, he is too sick to even groan. In the dark my hero brother looks so small and defenseless.

Mama puts wet towels in front of an open window in hopes a breeze will poke its way in to cool off the room. She forces him to drink tea and feeds him aspirin.

Before he's up and around, we all have the measles. Daddy's still working down south. "Stay there," Mama tells him on the phone when he tells her he doesn't remember if he had the measles.

My uncle delivers the new, old gas refrigerator. He sets it in the corner of the kitchen and lights the burner with a match. By suppertime we have cold milk and the next day we have ice cubes—*ice cubes!*

§

I love Ted, depend on him, and believe in him, but sometimes I can't stand his teasing. Like Daddy, he's sweet and loving one minute and violent the next. I fight back by throwing hairbrushes, plates, rocks, or whatever is handy, and then I run like hell for my life. If I can make it to Mama, I'm safe. I hide behind Mama and watch while he gets so mad, frustrated that he can't get me.

She tells him to go away and cool off. "Why do you fight with him? Why can't you just ignore him?" she asks me.

I try to rescue Mike from Ted when he picks on him and sometimes Bill. One day Mike picks up a Coke bottle and hits Ted square in the middle of his forehead, knocking him to the floor. Ted's head is bleeding and there's a huge knot growing where the bottle hit. Mama cleans up the blood, patches up his forehead and tells Ted, "Serves you right. Now maybe you'll leave him alone."

Ted is extremely good at sweet-talking Mama and me to get his way. One late afternoon, Ted starts arguing with Mama and he's losing. He's standing by the open back door getting ready to go milk the cows, and asking to go someplace when he gets done. Mama says, "No."

Bill, Mike and I watch shocked as Ted slaps her full in the face and knocks her to the floor. I don't know who is more stunned, him or her. He pulls back, the blood drains from his face, and he starts crying. "I'm sorry, I'm sorry. I didn't mean to do that. Please don't tell Dad."

Mama gets up looking shaky, her face white except for the red handprint on her cheek. She pulls her housedress straight and says, "Don't any of you kids tell Dad." We all know Daddy will hurt Ted, or worse, if he finds out about this.

Mama goes back to what she is doing and Ted goes to milk the cows. When Daddy comes in tired and dirty from the field, we talk and laugh at supper as usual. No one says a word about it to Daddy. We are used to keeping secrets from him, so what's one more in our Loony Tunes world?

Chapter Sixteen

In Love with Love

I get to go stay with my friend Joyce for a week; it sort of just happens. We are downtown on Saturday night and she says, "Why don't you come home with me?" I've done this before but only overnight and usually when I invite myself. Daddy isn't in favor of it, but Mama says, "Sure, go have a good time."

This is freedom. It is relief. It is luxury. They have running water, an actual bathroom, and electricity. Her mama is a quiet woman who says very little. Her dad is a big red-faced man by the name of Cletus, who wears bib overalls, and he never yells or says anything mean. He's like my daddy used to be. He speaks softly, and is always encouraging his five kids and giving them compliments.

Nobody ever talks nice to me like that anymore.

During those lazy, blistering-hot August days, Joyce and I ride horses up and down the road, talk about boys, share dreams and laugh. We watch curiously one morning as a fleet of gravel trucks come barreling down the road. Grabbing our horses, we go to check this situation out and see they are setting up shop near the grade school just south of her house. The next day they start ramming up the road heading north with trucks full of loose rock. The noise and dust make riding impossible.

We can see some of those gravel truck drivers are young and handsome. "How can we meet them?" I ask Joyce.

"Maybe they'd like a cold drink of water and some cookies."

"I bet they would."

First, we bake the cookies, then we fill a big jug with ice water. Finally, we make up a concoction of baby oil and iodine to spread all over our arms and legs. We put on Joyce's shortest shorts and skimpiest tops. My daddy would never allow me to wear short shorts or skimpy tops, but he's safely ten miles away.

We drag an old blanket and a bag of cookies and water out to the ditch by the road, and bring books so we'll look like sunbathers. We find a perfect place in the ditch with the fewest thistles, place our blanket at the right angle for the sun and wait, practicing the sexy poses we've seen Marilyn Monroe and Elizabeth Taylor do in the movies.

"How does this look?" Joyce giggles as she puts both hands behind her head with one knee up.

"Try lying on your side, and throwing one leg over the other."

We ignore the drivers until they honk, then we sit up wave, and show them the cookies and the water. Sometimes they stop and take a big drink and eat a cookie.

Leland is a husky blond god, in a T-shirt and tight jeans, who has a huge smile and a great laugh. He stops every day and my heart throbs so hard it nearly bounces out of my chest. At night I dream about Leland. Joyce says she does too, but I am sure he likes me better.

How did it happen? I didn't see it coming. One day boys are stupid, the next day boys are everything. Joyce confides in me about her crush on a boy in her school and I tell her about my dreams of having a husband, my own farm, and six babies. We are smitten with romance — in the movies, in books, and in the trashy magazines. We're hooked on the thought of romance like a heroin addict after his first needle. It all sounds so exquisitely delicious.

By now I know where babies come from, but I think every time you have sex you have a baby. I am sure I want to do sex at least six times!

On Saturday night we dress as nicely as is possible for farm girls. We're hoping we will "accidentally" run into the gravel truck drivers when we get to town. We look around but don't see any of them.

"Joyce, I'm going to run in the bar and let my daddy know I'm here." I walk in and see Leland having a beer with Daddy. *This is too good to be true.* I walk up and hug Daddy and Leland quickly walks away. Daddy doesn't act very glad to see me.

"Come on, we're leaving." *He's leaving a full beer this early in the evening?* I wave good-bye helplessly to Joyce as we walk out the door.

In the car, Daddy is furious. "What the hell is wrong with you? That guy was laughing with me about the two little girls laying in the ditch flirting with the gravel truck drivers. When you walked in, he said, 'There's one of them.'"

Daddy points his finger at me and shouts, "I'm not raising my daughter to be a whore."

I don't know what that is but it must be bad.

"It'll be a cold day in hell before you ever go stay with Joyce again. She's a bad influence. And take off those dangling earrings! Only chippies wear dangling earrings. Why can't you be a lady like your mother?"

All of this pours out of his mouth while I sit staring straight ahead and think *Go to hell.* Out loud I say, "Where's Mom?"

"Mike's sick; they stayed home."

"I wish I could live with Joyce. I wish I didn't have to go home at all."

I wait in silence but Daddy says nothing.

The next morning Mama says to me, "You sure know how to hurt your dad. He paced the floor all night over what you said to him. Do you have to be so ornery?"

"I'm not sorry," I fling at her, even though secretly I feel terrible about hurting Daddy.

I dream about Leland night after night for weeks and look for him every time we go to town. I see him once driving his truck downtown past the corner I am standing on. I wave and he waves.

Chapter Seventeen

The Big Freeze

We meet them in church, people we've never seen before. The whole congregation openly stares at them. Daddy says, "They must be the new family living on the farm west of us."

The dad is a tall man in a good-looking, gray three-piece suit.

Don't see that much around here.

His wife is much bigger than my mom—not fat, just big. She wears a beautiful red silk dress.

This family must have money.

There is a gawky girl about my age, and a pale-faced boy with almost colorless hair about Ted's age. Julie and Sam, they say when we talk to them after church.

They've arrived just in time to start school. This is excitement I've not known before—a girl my age in school. Ted and Sam are in the eighth grade. There's never been this many kids in our country school before. *Oh, this is going to be the best year ever!* Life takes on a whole new meaning. I am full of new enthusiasm, and eager to get up in the mornings and race off to school.

Julie and I share everything—secrets, dreams, lunches, homework, and console each other about our teasing big brothers.

I ride my horse to Julie's house on Sunday afternoons. They have a beautiful home. Julie is *sooo* lucky to live there. Her mom and dad are so nice. We play games, and include Sam in our activities. I am now twelve and Sam becomes the object of my passion and my romantic ideas. I no longer see a pale-faced, weak-looking blond who's not tough, strong, and handsome like dark curly-haired Ted. I see a boy who runs to meet me when I ride up, who helps me down from my horse, and who gives me his full attention when I talk.

I am *what-will-the-neighbors-think* mortified when they show up at our house one evening and see our shabby furniture and scratched up tables. We're all wrestling in the living room and the couch and chairs are pushed back, pillows are all over the place, and one even had stuffing hanging out of it.

They couldn't have come at a worse time. I hurry to try to put things back together, but it's too late, they've already seen it. *What are they thinking?*

Ted knows I have a crush on Sam. He says I am nutty, and teases me even worse. Funny thing about Ted, he can be so mean to me but he never wants me to be mad at him. If I am mad at him, he will do most anything to get back in my good graces. I learn to use this to my advantage.

Seventh grade is tough. Our new teacher, Miss Holmes, is a tall, athletic old maid of twenty years. The first day, in the cool school building that smells of floor wax, varnish, and scrubbed kids wearing Avon and

Brylcreem, she comes in all full of herself, obnoxious, and nasty.

"I've heard that the inmates are running the asylum at this school. Let me make this very clear. I have a belt and I know how to use it. I am in charge and don't ever doubt that I mean what I say."

She is mean to a skinny little Arnold, a first grader like Bernie. She cracks him across the head with a ruler for the least little thing and badgers him until he stutters. The more he stutters, the more she makes fun of him. She won't let him go to the outhouse so he wets his pants. She makes him do work at the blackboard so all can see the ugly wet stain running down the front of his pants.

My heart breaks for him. *She better not ever do this to Bernie.* It doesn't occur to me to tell his mother or even mine. Teachers are always right.

Miss Holmes makes second grader Beth so nervous she cries and twists her hair when she corrects her.

She torments us each in her own way. But she doesn't scare Ted. When she threatens him he looks at her with a sneer on his face. When she demands he go to the basement and fill the furnace with coal, he says, "What are you getting paid for?"

I never get a recess. When she rings the bell for a break, she always says, "Except you, Evelyn. You need to work on your spelling (or reading, math, or geography). Julie gets to go outside without me.

We'd been nailing up crepe paper streamers, getting ready for a spring school carnival. On Friday we still had some streamers and some posters to put up and Miss

Holmes couldn't find her hammer. She looks at Ted and says, "Why did you steal my hammer?" She looks at me and says, "What's the matter, can't your folks afford a hammer? I know you guys took it because it was here last night. Mike run home and get my hammer."

Mike came back empty-handed. Mom didn't know what he was talking about and understanding there was some need for a hammer said Dad had the hammer in the car, which Mike shared

"I knew it, you're just a bunch of thieves. You get that back here to me."

We went home for lunch and told Mama, "Miss Holmes accused us in front of the whole school of stealing her hammer."

Tight-lipped and hopping mad, Mama walks us back to school. I can hear Mama and the teacher talking in the hall. Coming back in the room, Miss Holmes twists her mouth up and remarks, "You didn't take it, huh?"

School is a courtroom and she's the judge, the jury, and the jailer.

§

I want money to buy Mama a present. She loves owls and I have some cute, pink and white, owl salt-and-pepper shakers picked out in the Sears catalog. They cost four dollars and ninety-five cents. I have to find something I can do to make money. Then I find an ad in the back of a comic book that says I can make a lot of money selling magazines and greeting cards. Secretly I

fill out the ad, and in no time, I have greeting card
samples and magazine flyers. Armed with this stuff on a
Saturday night in town, I corner relatives and neighbors.

I'm on a mission to make mama happy.

*Mama will be so surprised and so happy. She'll say
something like you're the best daughter in the world.*

The cards and magazines are mailed directly to the
buyer. I collect some of the money but before I can collect
the rest, winter hits. One blizzard hits and then another
and another with the full force of a thousand machine
guns.

Nobody gets to go anywhere except Daddy. He rides
one horse and uses another as a pack animal to bring
home groceries. He comes home full of snow, ice hanging
from his eyelashes, his face purple from the cold.
Sometimes he walks the four miles home hanging on to
the horse's tail because the snow is so deep, and the wind
blowing so hard that the horse can hardly walk.

When life gets really boring, we have taffy pulls.
Mama teaches us to make taffy the way she did as a kid.
Mike is really good at it, tossing the burning hot
stickiness from hand to hand like a pro. Daddy joins in
sometimes. We make popcorn balls, homemade potato
chips and cookies. We put whole onions in the red coals
in the stove. When it seems we've left them there long
enough, we gingerly pull them out with a bent coat
hanger, peel off the charred outside, and eat the middle
dripping in home-churned butter.

Daddy brings in the wooden ice-cream maker, and
ice from the frozen horse tank in a big gunny sack.

Mama mixes up cream, milk, raw eggs, sugar, and vanilla, and pours it in a silver cylinder that fits in the wooden shell. The crank top has to go on just right, then Daddy packs ice solidly around the cylinder, and pours a bunch of salt over it, and we take turns winding the handle.

"Is it done yet? Can we quit yet? Somebody else come and turn this for a while; my arms are tired."

"It's not done until it's frozen so hard you can't turn it anymore."

The milky snowdrifts are so high that Daddy has to climb out an upstairs window and shovel a path to the door. A couple of times he has to tie a rope from the house to the barn so he and Ted can find their way back—the horses and old Bessie needs to be fed. The potbellied iron stove in the living room is working overtime. Sometimes the stove pipe turns a bright glowing red. The piles of wood leaning against the wall have to be refilled twice a day.

Mike backs up to the stove too far and burns all the skin off his butt. We can't take him to town. Mama has him lying on the couch with Vaseline heaped on the burn. They worry that he might get an infection so no one can go near him for a while. He never complains and doesn't cry. Eventually we sit on the floor by the couch and play cards with him. He makes up tall stories and has us all laughing—the imaginations of his mind are incredible. *Who can think up stuff like this?*

For me this winter is especially good—even though it's hard to stay warm and even though the poop in the upstairs pot freezes solid. Daddy stays home. Nights, he puts a mattress on the floor in the living room, piles it high with blankets, and we all sleep near the stove. I'm surrounded by warm bodies. We are not only close, we're practically on top of each other.

The voices stop torturing me and I feel safe.

The snow piles up to our second story window.

"Just think if you fell in there, no one would ever find you until spring," Ted tells me when Mama sends us upstairs to bring something down.

"Maybe it's a good thing we can't get the window open."

There is no school more often than not as Miss Holmes can't make it there. When she does, she rides her horse. One call on the party line is all it takes to let us know if there's going to be school or not.

On a Saturday in April the snow is still so deep we can't take a car or a wagon to town and Easter is the next day.

Mama is wringing her hands.

"What's wrong, Mama?"

"The little kids won't get anything from the Easter Bunny. Your dad rode into town yesterday and he's not home yet."

"Why don't you let me take the pinto to town and get some Easter stuff."

"I don't have any money."

"I could go collect my card money from Aunt Dorothy and buy them something."

"Oh, I don't know if that's a good idea."

"Please, Mama, I can do it."

"Maybe I should send Ted with you."

Overhearing, Ted announces, "I'm not going."

"Okay, then go saddle the horse for her."

Looking directly at me, Mama says, "You get home as fast as you can."

She gives me a worried look as I pull on my coat and scarf, warm checkered flannel mittens she made out of one of Daddy's old shirts, two pairs of socks, my brown oxfords and finally a pair of black high-buckle overshoes.

Ted groans and complains but he saddles the horse. I get on feeling scared but daring and purposeful. *I can do this.* My feet in the stirrups almost touch the snow as I ride down the road in the sunshine. The snowplow made one pass through just before the last blizzard, so at least I can see where the road is supposed to be. I sing and talk to myself all the way to Aunt Dorothy's house on the edge of town. She is surprised to see me.

"How'd you get here?"

"Rode my horse."

"Come in and get warm. Why are you here?"

I stammer, "Um, I um, remember, um, the greeting cards?" I can hardly get the words out. I'm embarrassed to ask for the money. I stutter, "I, uh, I need to . . . to . . . to collect." I finally spit it out with great relief.

Aunt Dorothy gives me a five dollar bill for a three dollar box of cards.

"Thank you," I say my heart sinking, "but I don't have change."

"That's okay. You come back here now if you need anything else." That's what I love about her.

In town I tie my horse to the little tree beside Burn's General Store and walk confidently in feeling proud of my newfound role. I carefully consider what would be the best thing to buy. There's candy bunnies and candy sticks, chocolates wrapped in Easter paper, and jars of licorice. There's even some licorice pipes and some tin Easter bunnies that hop when you wind them up. I look at it all and choose bags of soft pink and yellow chickens and bunnies, some jelly beans, wind-up rabbits for Bill and Bernie, a monkey beating a drum for Mike, a chocolate bunny for each of us.

Proudly, I lay the money on the counter. Jack, the store owner, hands me back a nickel. *I can have a bottle of orange pop.* We're forbidden to drink Coke, and even though no one will know, I can't do it.

The road leading home is cold and deserted and white as far as I can see. Even the fenceposts are covered with snow. It's almost dusk. Houses way back from the road have gray smoke coming out of the chimneys.

I feel strangely triumphant. *I doing it by myself.* I sing songs and try not to hear the voices that jeer at me that something bad is going to happen. *You didn't buy the right stuff. You could fall off this horse and never get up. You wore the wrong clothes to town. Aunt Dorothy doesn't really like you. Mama won't be happy with what you bought.*

The closer we get to home, the more the pinto wants to run. I hold her back, afraid of losing my bags in the snow. Finally, I trot into the driveway carrying my booty. Mama's face shines with relief when I walk in. I know it's because now the little kids will have the joy of believing in the Easter Bunny' s visit.

The house is warm and smells like homemade bread. Lined up on the table are decorated Easter baskets made out of cut-off cereal boxes with colored pictures cut from magazines pasted on them, and braided rags for handles. The excitement on their faces makes it all worthwhile. Plus, now I am a grown-up—in on the secret.

Daddy is at breakfast. He brought a box of chocolates for Mama and balloons for the kids. It's really killing Mama that we can't go to church. "I haven't been out of this house for seventeen weeks," she tells me while she makes whipped frosting for a three-layer cake for our special Easter dinner. She decorates the cake, making little nests out of the brightly colored jelly beans I bought. At least this much is the same as every other year. Mama has such a talent for making something out of nothing.

Daddy is funny when it comes to food. He wants to make sure we eat well and everyone has enough. He never takes a second helping without holding up the plate or bowl and asking, "Anyone need more of this?" He won't touch his dessert until he asks, "Anybody want this?" Mama gets upset with him for this sometimes.

"You eat it, you need it more than they do."

"No, no, no, let them eat all they want first."

No mention is made, or questions asked about where Daddy has been for the last forty-eight hours, at least not when I'm around.

Chapter Eighteen

Visitors

A month past my thirteenth birthday, the boys and I are playing Captain, May I? in the hot July dust of the front yard. We watch as an old Chevy with a Michigan license plate pulls up to our door. Mom, who's in the garden, stands up, brushes the dirt off her housedress and comes to see who it is.

A man, possibly twenty-something, crawls out of the driver's seat. "Will he bite?" he asks about our barking dog.

"Nah," Ted says, "He's harmless."

"Does Lon Jones live here?"

"He's out in the field. Can I help you?" Mom says.

"I need to talk to him; it's important."

"Come on in, have some tea. Ted will have to go get him."

"No, we'll just wait in the car."

"Who are they?" I ask Mama who has started cooking supper.

"I've no idea. I've never seen them before."

I watch out the window as Dad walks up to the car, talks briefly, shakes hands with all of them and brings them to the door. I hear Dad say, "Put on some extra plates, Mom, we have company for supper. This is Charley, his wife Donna, and Pete."

Oh, I know Mama doesn't like Daddy to call her Mom.

We sit around the table talking and laughing. Charlie obviously knows Daddy well. They talk about things in Missouri, but the mystery of who they are, and what they want, hangs in the air like a phantom bumble bee.

The next morning, I ask again, "Who are they? Are they cousins?"

"No," Mama says.

"Then who are they?" I persist.

"Just some friends of your dad's."

They stay for a month. Charlie helps Dad do chores and work in the fields. Ted gets a reprieve from his duties and hangs out with Pete who is about his age. They do fun stuff like swim in the stock dam, ride horses, and hike to town. I'm envious of them.

Donna sleeps in, polishes her nails, and asks me to brush her long black hair. She shares her *Glamour* magazines with me. She isn't very happy about having to go to the bathroom in a stinky wooden outhouse, or take a bath in a small round tin tub.

"How do you do it?" she asks me.

They don't seem to be in any hurry to leave. We eat a lot of watermelon, play a lot of softball, and do our best to stay cool. When other family members show up at our house, Charlie, Donna, and Pete just sort of blend in like they belong. Charlie has black hair and brilliant blue-green eyes. I'm amazed at how much he looks like Daddy. I like him a lot.

Charlie thanks Mama over and over again as they walk out the door carrying their suitcases. It's been a fun month having them here. The mystery of who they are still hangs in the air as they pull out of the driveway. I know there is more to this story.

"Ted, did Pete say anything to you about who they are?"

"No. What does it matter?"

Chapter Nineteen

Watching My Back

On Labor Day, Julie invites me to go with their family to the county fair. I get to sit in the back seat in the middle between her and Sam. I'm in seventh heaven as Sam holds my hand and the three of us talk and laugh during the thirty-mile ride.

A flat field at the edge of Gettysburg has been turned into a wonderland. Lights are strung over booths that hold games and food. Red, blue, green, and yellow florescent tubes light up carnival rides, and loud music booms. The horses on the merry-go-round bob up and down. The Ferris wheel calls our names, and our excitement pulls us laughing and joking down the midway.

I've never been to a fair before, though I have been to the yearly carnival called Old Settlers Picnic we have in Seneca every summer. We kids are in the parade every year. Sometimes we win enough money to pay for the carnival rides. When we don't, Daddy gives us each a dollar to spend on the ten-cent rides and the nickel cotton candy.

Now I'm with my friends, all grown-up, with five dollars to spend. We race up and down the midway.

Somehow, I lose everyone and wander around the fair searching for them. *Where can they be? We were all walking together.* I just stopped and said hi to Joyce and suddenly they were gone.

At the edge of the fair near the barn I see their dad who is looking for me.

"I lost Sam and Julie."

"They're in the car," he says, putting his arm around my shoulder. The sweaty, sweet smell of his cologne hits my nose as he backs me up toward the barn. Confused and afraid, my gut feels like it's been stomped by a pair of combat boots.

"You have a nice body," he murmurs as he starts feeling my tender breasts and running his hands up and down my back, over my butt, and between my legs. I stand as still as a petrified tree in a forest and let him rub his hands all over me. When a laughing, shouting gaggle of people come our way, he sort of pushes me toward the path and we walk the short distance to the car.

In the car Sam reaches for my hand and it lies limp in his. Sick to my stomach with fear and disbelief, I swallow and swallow, and swallow some more, to keep from throwing up. *I just want out of this car. I just want to go home. I just want to never see this family again.*

The ride home is silent and seems to take forever. I sit still as a stone as Sam falls asleep with his head on my shoulder.

At home Mama is reading the Bible again. Barely looking up, she asks, "Did you have a nice time?"

"Just fine, Mama."

"Well, go to bed. It's late and school starts tomorrow. Aren't you excited?"

I follow my ritual of kissing her on the cheek before bed. "Good night, Mom."

"Don't forget to say your prayers."

Right . . . a lot of good that does.

A couple of days later Julie's father comes to pick her up from school. He finds me alone in the entryway by the stone watercooler. He pushes me against the wall. I pull away, escaping into the safety of Miss Holmes' company in the main room.

"You still here?" she says. I pretend like I'm looking for something in my desk. *I will never go to Julie's house again.* There is now an unscalable wall between Julie and me, even though I try to pretend it never happened.

In spite of constantly having to watch my back, life is exciting. Eighth grade holds promise. Sam and Ted are going twenty-five miles away to Faulkton High School. Julie and I are the oldest kids in our school. Miss Holmes is still the teacher. I still don't get any recesses, but she has to let me go home for lunch.

Daddy still works for old Mr. Barnes. One night he comes home with a face full of buckshot. He says he was hunting from the car and the gun blew up. Mama picks lead pellets out of his face, neck, and shoulder and dabs at the blood with peroxide.

§

I'm not sure when I start fantasizing about being an orphan. Sometimes I think of how nice it would be to live somewhere else with someone else. Maybe my parents will get killed in a car accident on the way home some night and then I can go live with people who will love me. It'll be a happier place where there is a bathroom with running water and electric lights.

Then I feel gobbled up by guilt and I think God will punish me for these pea-brained thoughts. The guilt eats at me like maggots feasting through a pile of dung. Often, I have nightmares and monster dreams.

Sometimes in my dreams I see something terrible happen to Mama. To make it up to her for all this horrible thinking, I force myself to pay attention to her moods and anticipate her wants. I do things for her that she finds annoying, like trying to help her iron our clothes. We have a gas iron that runs on little canisters of propane. It needs to be handled very carefully or Mama says it will explode. Once when it was sitting there while she ran to do something else, I picked it up to iron my own shirt.

"Stop!" she yells.

"I'm just trying to help."

"It won't help if you get blown-up."

I'm in trouble so much of the time because I say straightforward and true things in a home where secrets and mind reading are sacred. I'm in the wrong if I question the crazy behavior. I get yelled at for noticing that Daddy is woozy, and I'm told not to tattle on my brothers. Mama doesn't want to hear anything unpleasant. She says, "Don't ever come to me with stories about your brothers, or they will never trust you."

§

Early one Friday night Daddy comes home from the Barnes farm fuming mad. It's payday, and he's been shorted $100.00. The gun that blew up in his face belonged to Mr. Barnes.

"Can you believe he wants me to pay for that gun? Can you believe it?" I can hear Mama and Daddy's murmuring voices long after I am in bed.

Saturday morning, I'm almost at the bottom of the stairs when I hear Daddy yell. Peeking around the door, I see Mr. Barnes standing just inside the back door. He says something and Daddy dives for the woodbox, picks up a small log, and yells, "Get out!"

I see Mr. Barnes put his hands in the air, and wheel around to make a quick exit. Daddy follows him out and in minutes I hear a car zoom out the driveway. Venturing out to the table, I sit quietly, knowing better than to ask questions.

§

Some of Ted's friends came out to the farm. It's Sunday afternoon and there's nothing to do. They drive up in a Jeep with the top down and ask Ted and me if we want to go for a ride. We jump in and take off down the dusty bumpy road singing and yelling at the top of our lungs. We race up, around, and cross country for fifteen or twenty miles.

When we get home, I'm caught off guard by Mama's anger. "Mama it's just Willie, Morris, and Dick. We all go to church together. What's wrong with them?"

"There is nothing wrong with them, it's you racing around the countryside with four boys, your hair flying, and screaming at the top of your lungs. You look like a delinquent barbarian. Look at your hair now and your face is full of dirt. Where is your common sense? Ladies don't act this way! What are people going to think of us?"

"Well, they might think we are having fun."

"Don't you talk back to me, young lady! This is a small town. Everybody knows everybody's business."

Chapter Twenty

Moving On

High school is a whole new ball of wax—a couple of hundred kids instead of the ten I'm used to. I love the atmosphere and the challenge. I rarely see Julie and Sam even though we go to the same high school. That's okay. My appreciation for them is dampened, although secretly I still like Sam.

Ted already has a lot of friends in our high school and is on the football team. I make new friends the first day. Our math teacher forbids girls to wear jeans in his classroom. He says, "Some of you girls in jeans should see yourselves in a rearview mirror."

We agree that he's an ogre. Someone says, "Yeah, well his butt isn't all that great from behind either." But we don't want to flunk algebra so we stop wearing jeans.

My first school dance is a hoot. I've never danced before but it doesn't matter. Shy guys approach me nervously and I dance with them. One of Ted's football friends comes over. We slow dance to *Unchained Melody*—I am Cinderella and he is the prince. Later, Ted jeers at me and tells me Alex said, "Boy, your sister sure likes to dance close."

I have a job in the school lunchroom collecting the lunch money. For doing this they give me free lunches.

They also pay me one dollar a day but they don't know it. Stealing is my way of getting spending money. All the kids meet at the soda shop for root beer floats and now I can join them.

The clothes I wear to school belonged to somebody before me and my underwear is ragged. One day I am walking across the lunchroom in a dress that doesn't look too bad when the elastic waistband on my underpants snaps. My underpants hit the floor. Mortified, I dive after them and gather them up under my full skirt. I race for the bathroom, throw them in the trash, and go without panties for the rest of the day. No underwear under my full skirt feels really weird as I self-consciously walk from class to class.

Did anyone see me? If they noticed I will never live it down. Nobody says anything so I guess everybody was too busy eating to watch me walk across the floor.

I hang around football practice waiting for Ted every day. One afternoon after school Ted hands me the keys to the pick-up and says, "Here's the keys, I'm not going home."

"I don't know how to drive, you idiot."

"You can do it if you want to; it's easy. Anyway, you have to, because I'm not going home."

I hang out at football practice until I see one of the town kids from Seneca. He's a big senior I used to go to Bible school with. "I'm stranded, I don't know where my brother is and I need somebody to drive the pick-up."

He looks at me with pity. "Yeah I spose. Where are you parked?" I'm silently wishing Ted in hell all the way home, but sort of pleased to be with this guy. He has his hand on the floor gearshift knob. I lay my hand on top of his—flirting a bit. He ignores me. It's dark by the time we get to the farm.

Daddy thanks him for taking care of me and drives him to his house in town, then he goes looking for Ted. They get home about midnight. I hear Dad tell Mom, "This isn't working. We have to move to a town where there is work and a high school. My kids will go to high school. I never got beyond the fourth grade. That is not going to happen to my kids. We need to start looking for a place to move."

§

I love, adore, and treasure my pesky brothers, all who seem to love me back—at least most of the time. There was a time I could make them do what I wanted by being more powerful than them. Now they are bigger and stronger and I have to learn a new way to deal with them. Might doesn't always make right, especially if you're only five feet tall and weigh one hundred and twenty pounds.

Most of the time I protect myself from Dad's barbs by acting like I'm invincible. Always in the back of my mind is a fear of a powerful God who, if He wants to, can, knock me or someone I love dead in a heartbeat.

One night at supper Dad says, "We are going to make this move as quietly as possible so don't you kids talk about it at school or anywhere else." Mom says, "I'm not going to tell my Club or anyone at Ladies Aid. I don't want them to have a big going away party for me. This is only a temporary move, we will be back this summer. In fact, we are going to spend all our summers at the farm." This gives me hope and confusion at the same time. Now I don't know what to think about this move. It's exciting to be going and the thought of coming back for the summer is comforting.

I feel lucky that my father wants me to graduate from high school. A lot of farmers in our area make their daughters drop out of school after eighth grade. I've heard a neighbor say "Boys are the only ones who need an education as they are the ones who have to support a family". My dad often says "Evelyn, you are going to have an education and learn to take care of yourself. Hell if I have my way you're even going to college like your mother." Sometimes I can't stand my dad, and other times I long to throw my arms around him and beg for forgiveness, even though I don't know what I've done to him. I love him and then sometimes I hate him.

I love school and I will miss all my friends. That's okay I tell myself, I'll make new friends and then I'll have friends here and friends there. I can't know the danger that is ahead and the destruction that slowly eats away at our family. What's ahead for freckled-faced, red-headed, half-baked me with a heart full of love and a head full of fear? I'm shivery with anticipation.

Post Script

In the 1950s girls had one goal—to marry well. The highest position a girl held in business was secretary, and that was only until she married. Then it was her job to produce children, make her husband happy, and always live by The Ten Commandments, especially the fifth one: 'Honor thy father and thy mother."

From overhearing my mother talk with her sisters and the neighbors I've learned women have to be virgins and not shame the family by getting pregnant. And if they never get married they must stay virgins. I understand any woman not married before she is twenty will be an old maid—which to hear them talk is a fate worse than death. I know it's a girl's job to have a cedar hope chest filled with linens, that we make our mothers look good, and fulfill her dreams by having a beautiful house, gorgeous china, and a place in society. A girl's greatest challenge is to be an excellent wife and mother.

I asked my mother "What about your cousin Evelyn, the woman I'm named after? She owns her own band uniform factory." With a shake of her head she replied "Yes but her husband had to die for that to be possible. Ladies do what they have to do."

I can't know the danger ahead and the destruction that continues to build for our family.

Author's Note

When I started my journey as an author, I didn't have the full vision for the *Blood, Sex, and Tears* series, I now have. This book is number 4 in the series, based on the order of publication. To read my story in sequence the order is:

Just Fine Thank You
My life from a young girl through age thirteen

Dance Like There's No Tomorrow (Forthcoming*)*
My life as a young woman through age eighteen

To Be Somebody (Revised 2019)
My life as a young married woman through age thirty.

The next book in the series will be about my process of looking at my losses and finding serenity. I share my story from early childhood through recovery to reveal how dysfunction in families continues from one generation to another, unless there is an intentional effort to break the cycle. It's my desire that you can find hope for yourself or a loved one based on my story of redemption.

About the Author

Evelyn M. Leite, MHR, LPC professional counselor and author, has thirty-five years of experience in the addiction and mental health fields. Noted for her humanitarian work, she was inducted into the South Dakota Hall of Fame in 2008.

She is widely regarded for her seminars in counseling and education. She has designed and implemented relationship programs throughout the United States and is recognized for her success in the treatment of grief, trauma resolution, and codependency. She has authored dozens of articles, and is published by Hazelden Publications of Center City Minnesota as well as the former Johnson Institute.

In addition to this book, her best works are *Women: What Do We Want?* and *A Fix for the Family Rift Caused by*

Addiction, published by Living With Solutions Press, Rapid City, South Dakota.

Your feedback is welcome!

I welcome your letters and feedback to this book please find me on Facebook under LIVING WITH SOLUTIONS or write to me at PO Box 9702, Rapid City, SD 57709

Other books by Evelyn Leite, MHR, LPC

If you enjoyed this book by Evelyn Leite, MHR, LPC, you might enjoy these, also part of the *Blood, Sex, and Tears* series:

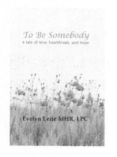

To Be Somebody (Living With Solutions, Rapid City, SD 2014, Rev. 2019) Book 1 in the Blood, Sex, and Tears series.
ISBN: 978-1733540926

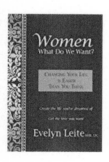

Women: What Do We Want? Changing your life is easier than you think (Living With Solutions, Rapid City, SD 2015, Rev. 2019)
ISBN: 978-1733540940

A Fix for the Rift in the Family Caused by Addiction (Living With Solutions, Rapid City, SD 2018) Book 3 in the *Blood, Sex, and Tears* series
ISBN: 978-1733540919

Beyond the series, Evelyn offers:

Detachment (Johnson Institute Minneapolis, MN 1980, Hazelden Publications, Center City MN 1986).

Granite Island Amber Sea, Day at the Rally (Black Hills Writers Press, Rapid City, South Dakota, 2012)

A Sunday From Innocence (Black Hills Writers Press, Black Hills Literary Journal, Rapid City, South Dakota, 2013)

Available internationally through quality online retailers.

Made in the USA
Monee, IL
09 August 2020